MAKING THE MOST OF LIFE
J.R. Miller

A Word of Introduction.

To have the gift of life is a solemn thing. Life is God's most sacred trust. It is not ours to do with as we please; it must be accounted for—every particle, every power, every possibility of it.

These chapters are written with the purpose and hope of stimulating those who may read them to earnest and worthy living. If they seem urgent, if they present continually motives of thoughtfulness, if they dwell almost exclusively on the side of obligation and responsibility, if they make duty ever prominent and call to self-renunciation and self-sacrifice, leaving small space for play—it is because life itself is really most serious, and because we must meet it seriously, recognizing its sacred meaning and girding ourselves for it with all earnestness and energy.

If this book shall teach any how to make the most of the life God has entrusted to them, that will be reward enough for the work of its preparation. To this service it is affectionately dedicated, in the name of Him who made the most of his blessed life—by losing it in love's sacrifice, and who calls us also to die to self that we may live unto God.

J. R. Miller

Chapter 1. Making the Most of Life.

"Then Jesus said to his disciples—If anyone would come after me, he must deny himself and take up his cross and follow me. For whoever wants to save his life will lose it—but whoever loses his life for me will find it. What good will it be for a man if he gains the whole world, yet forfeits his soul? Or what can a man give in exchange for his soul?" Matthew 16:24-26

According to our Lord's teaching, we can make the most of our life by losing it. He says that losing the life for his sake is saving it. There is a *lower self* that must be trampled down and trampled to death by the *higher self*. The alabaster vase must be broken, that the ointment may flow out to fill the house. The grapes must be *crushed*—that there may be wine to drink. The wheat must be *bruised*—before it can become bread to feed hunger.

It is so in life. *Whole, unbruised, unbroken men* are of but little use. True living is really a succession of battles, in which the better triumphs over the worse, the spirit over the flesh. Until we cease to live for *self*—we have not begun to live at all.

We can never become truly useful and helpful to others, until we have learned this lesson. One may live for self and yet do many pleasant things for others; but one's life can never become the great blessing to the world it was meant to be—until the law of self-sacrifice has become its heart principle.

A great oak stands in the forest. It is beautiful in its majesty; it is ornamental; it casts a pleasant shade. Under its branches the children play; among its boughs the birds sing. One day the woodman comes with his axe, and the tree quivers in all its branches, under his sturdy blows. "I am being destroyed!" it cries. So it seems, as the great tree crashes down to the ground. And the children are sad because they can play no more beneath the broad branches; the birds grieve because they can no more nest and sing amid the summer foliage.

But let us follow the tree's history. It is cut into boards, and built into a beautiful cottage, where human hearts find their happy nest. Or it is used in making a great organ which leads the worship of a congregation. The losing of its life was the saving of it. It died that it might become deeply, truly useful.

The plates, cups, dishes, and vases which we use in our homes and on our tables, once lay as common clay in the earth, quiet and restful—but in no way doing good, serving man. Then came men with picks, and the clay was harshly torn out and plunged into a mortar and beaten, and ground in a mill, then pressed, and then put into a furnace, and burned and burned, at last coming forth in beauty, and beginning its history of usefulness. It was apparently *destroyed* that it might begin to be of service.

A great church-building is going up, and the stones that are being laid on the walls are brought out of the dark quarry for this purpose. We can imagine them complaining, groaning, and repining, as the quarry men's drills and hammers struck them. They supposed they were being *destroyed* as they were torn out from the bed of rock where they had lain undisturbed for ages, and were cut into blocks, and lifted out, and then as they were chiseled and dressed into form. But they were being *destroyed* only that they might become *useful*. They become part of a new sanctuary, in which God is to be worshiped, where the Gospel will be preached, where penitent sinners will find the Christ-Savior, where sorrowing ones will be comforted. Surely it was better that these stones should be torn out, even amid agony, and built into the wall of the church, than that they should have lain ages more, undisturbed in the dark quarry. They were saved from *uselessness,* by being *destroyed.*

These are simple illustrations of the law which applies also in human life. We must die to be useful—to be truly a blessing. Our Lord put this truth in a little parable, when he said that the seed must fall into the earth and die that it may bear fruit. Christ's own cross is the highest illustration of this. His friends said he wasted his precious life; but was that life wasted when Jesus was crucified?

People said that Harriet Newell's beautiful life was wasted when she gave it to missions, and then died and was buried far from home—bride, missionary, mother, saint, all in one short year—without even telling to one heathen woman or child the story of the Savior. But was that lovely young life indeed wasted? No; all this century her name has been one of the strongest inspirations to missionary work, and her influence has brooded everywhere, touching thousands of hearts of gentle women and strong men, as the story of her consecration has been told. Had Harriet Newell lived a thousand years of quiet, sweet life at home, she could not have done the work that she did in one short year by giving her life, as it seemed, an unavailing sacrifice. She lost her life that she might save it. She died that she might live. She offered herself a living sacrifice that she might become useful.

In heart and spirit we must all do the same if we would ever be a real blessing in the world. We must be willing to lose our life—to sacrifice ourself, to give up our own way, our own ease, our own comfort, possibly even our own life; for there come times when one's life must literally be lost in order to be saved.

There is more grandeur in five minutes of self-renunciation, than in a whole lifetime of self-interest and self-seeking. There is something Christly in it. How poor, paltry, and mean, alongside the records of such deeds, appear men's selfish strivings, self-interests' boldest venturing!

We must get the same spirit in us if we would become in any large and true sense a blessing to the world. We must die to live. We must lose our life to save it. We must lay self on the altar to be consumed in the fire of love, in order to glorify God and do good to men. Our work may be fair, even though mingled with self; but it is only when self is sacrificed, burned on the altar of consecration, consumed in the hot flames of love, that our work becomes really our best, a fit offering to be made to our King.

We must not fear that in such sacrifice, such renunciation and annihilation of self, we shall lose ourselves. God will remember every deed of love, every forgetting of self, every emptying out of life. Though we work in obscurest places, where no human tongue shall ever voice our praise, still there is a record kept, and some day rich and glorious reward will be given. Is not God's praise better than man's?

Mary's ointment was wasted when she broke the vase and poured it upon her Lord. Yes; but suppose she had left the ointment in the unbroken vase? What remembrance would it then have had? Would there have been any mention of it on the Gospel pages? Would her deed of careful keeping have been told over all the world? She broke the vase and poured it out, lost it, sacrificed it, and now the perfume fills all the earth. We may keep our life if we will, carefully preserving it from waste; but we shall have no reward, no honor from it, at the last. But if we empty it out in loving service, we shall make it a lasting blessing to the world, and we shall be remembered forever.

Chapter 2. Laid on God's Altar.

"Therefore, I urge you, brothers, in view of God's mercy, to offer your bodies as **living sacrifices**, holy and pleasing to God." Romans 12:1

We have to die to live. That is the central law of life. We must *burn* to give light to the world, or to give forth fragrance of incense to God's praise. We cannot save ourselves and at the same time make anything worthy of our life, or be in any deep and true sense an honor to God and a blessing to the world. The *altar* stands in the foreground of every life, and can be passed by only at the cost of all that is noblest and best.

All the practical side of true religion, is summed up in the exhortation of Paul, that we present our bodies a living sacrifice to God. Anciently, a man brought a lamb and presented it to God, laid it on the altar, to be consumed by God's fire. In like manner, we are to present our bodies. The first thing is not to be a worker, a preacher, a saver of souls; the very first thing in a Christian life is to present one's self to God, to lay one's self on the altar. We need to understand this. It is easier to talk and *work* for Christ—than to *give* ourselves to him. It is easier to offer God a few activities—than to give him our heart. But the heart must be first, else even the largest gifts and services are not acceptable.

"A living sacrifice." A sacrifice is something really given to God, to be his altogether and forever. We cannot take it back any more. One could not lay a lamb on God's altar and then a minute or two afterward run up and take it off. We cannot be God's today and our own tomorrow. If we become his at all, in a sacrifice which he accepts, we are his always.

How can we present ourselves as a sacrifice to God? By the complete surrender of our heart and will and all our powers to him. Absolute obedience is consecration. The soldier learns it. He is not his own. He does not think for himself, to, make his own plans; he has but one duty—to obey. Payson used to talk of his "lost will"— lost in God's will, he meant. That is what presenting one's self a sacrifice means.

It is a "living" sacrifice. Anciently, the sacrifices were killed; they were laid dead on the altar. We are to present ourselves living. The fire consumed the ancient offering; the fire of God's love and of his Spirit consumes our lives by purifying them and filling them with divine life. Those on whom the fire fell on the day of Pentecost, became new men. There was a new life in their souls, a new ardor, a new enthusiasm. They were on fire with love for Christ. They entered upon a service in which all their energies flamed.

The living sacrifice includes all the life—not what it is now only—but all that it may become. Life is not a diamond—but a seed, with possibilities of endless growth. Lyman Abbott has used this illustration: "I pluck an acorn from the greensward, and hold it to my ear; and this is what it says to me: 'By and by the birds will come and nest in me. By and by I will furnish shade for the cattle. By and by I will provide warmth for the home in the pleasant fire. By and by I will be shelter from the storm to those who have gone under the roof. By and by I will be the strong ribs of the great vessel, and the tempest will beat against me in vain, while I carry men across the Atlantic.' 'O foolish little acorn, will you be all this?' I ask. And the acorn answers, 'Yes; God and I.'"

I look into the faces of a company of children, and I hear a whisper, saying: "By and by I will be a great blessing to many. By and by other lives will come and find nest and home in me. By and by the weary will sit in the shadow of my strength. By and by I will sit as comforter in a home of sorrow. By and by I will speak the words of Christ's salvation in ears of lost ones. By and by I will shine in the full radiancy of the beauty of Christ, and be among the glorified with my Redeemer." "You, frail, powerless, little one?" I ask; and the answer is, "Yes; Christ and I." And all these blessed possibilities that are in the life of the young person, must go upon the altar in the living sacrifice.

Take another view of it. Some people seem to suppose that only spiritual exercises are included in this living sacrifice; that it does not cover their business, their social life, their amusements. But it really embraces the whole of life. We belong to God as truly on Monday as on the Lord's Day. We must keep ourselves laid on God's altar as really while we are at our week-day work as when we are in a prayer-meeting. We are always *on duty* as Christians, whether we are engaged in our secular pursuits or in exercises of devotion. All our work should therefore be done reverently, "as unto the Lord."

We should do everything also for God's eye and according to the principles of righteousness. The consecrated *mechanic* must put absolute truth into every piece of work he does. The consecrated *business man* must conduct his business on the principles of divine righteousness. The consecrated *millionaire* must lay his money on God's altar, so that every dollar of it shall do business for God, blessing the world. The consecrated *housekeeper* must keep her home so sweet and so tidy and beautiful all the days, that she would never be ashamed for her Master to come in without warning to be her guest. That is, when we present ourselves to God as a living sacrifice, we are to be God's in every part and in every phase of our life— wherever we go, whatever we do.

"I cannot be of any use," says one. "I cannot talk in meetings. I cannot pray in public. I have no gift for visiting the sick. There is nothing I can do for Christ."

Well, if Christian service were all talking and praying in meetings, and visiting the sick—it would be discouraging to such talentless people. But are our *tongues* the only faculties we can use for Christ? There are ways in which even *silent* people can belong to God and be a blessing in the world. A *star* does not talk—but its calm, steady beam shines down continually out of the sky, and is a benediction to many. A *flower* cannot sing bird-songs—but its sweet beauty and gentle fragrance make it a blessing wherever it is seen. Be like a *star* in your peaceful shining, and many will thank God for your life. Be like the *flower* in your pure beauty and in the influence of your unselfish spirit, and you may do more to bless the world than many who talk incessantly. The living sacrifice does not always mean *active* work. It may mean the patient endurance of a wrong, the quiet bearing of a pain; or cheerful acquiescence in a disappointment.

There are some people who think it impossible in their narrow sphere and in their uncongenial circumstances, to live so as to win God's favor or be blessings in the world. But there is no doubt that many of the most beautiful lives of earth, in God's sight, are those that are lived in what seem the most unfavorable conditions.

A visitor to Amsterdam wished to hear the wonderful music of the chimes of St. Nicholas, and went up into the tower of the church to hear it. There he found a man with wooden gloves on his hands, pounding on a keyboard. All he could hear was the clanging of the keys when struck by the wooden hammer, and the harsh, deafening noise of the bells close over his head. He wondered why people talked of the marvelous chimes of St. Nicholas. To his ear there was no music in them, nothing but terrible clatter and clanging. Yet, all the while, there floated out over and beyond the city the most entrancing music. Men in the fields paused in their work to listen and were made glad. People in their homes and travelers on the highways were thrilled by the marvelous bell-notes that fell from the chimes.

There are many lives, which to those who dwell close beside them, seem to make no music. They pour out their strength in hard toil. They are shut up in narrow spheres. They dwell amid the noise and clatter of common task-work. They appear to be only striking wooden hammers on rattling, noisy keys. There can be nothing pleasing to God in their life, men would say. They think themselves that they are not of any use, that no blessing goes out from their life. They never dream that sweet music is made anywhere in the world by their noisy hammering. As the bell-chimer in his little tower hears no music from his own ringing of the bells, so they think of their hard toil as producing nothing but clatter and clangor; but out over the world where the influence goes from their work and character, human lives are blessed, and weary ones hear with gladness sweet, comforting music. Then away off in heaven, where angels listen for earth's melody, most entrancing strains are heard!

No doubt it will be seen at the last—that many of earth's most acceptable living sacrifices have been laid on the altar in the narrowest spheres and in the midst of the hardest conditions. What to the ears of close listeners is only the noise of painful toil is heard in heaven as music as sweet as angels' song.

The living sacrifice is "acceptable unto God." It ought to be a wondrous inspiration to know this; that even the lowliest things we do for Christ are pleasing to him. We ought to be able to do better, truer work, when we think of his gracious acceptance of it. It is told of Leonardo da Vinci, that while still a pupil, before his *genius* burst into *brilliancy*, he received a special inspiration in this way: His old and famous master, because of his growing infirmities of age, felt obliged to give up his own work, and one day bade Da Vinci finish for him a picture which he had begun. The young man had such a reverence for his master's skill that he shrank from the task. The old artist, however, would not accept any excuse—but persisted in his command, saying simply, "Do your best."

Da Vinci at last tremblingly seized the brush and kneeling before the easel prayed: "It is for the sake of my beloved master that I implore skill and power for this undertaking." As he proceeded, his hand grew steady, his eye awoke with slumbering genius. He forgot himself and was filled with enthusiasm for his work. When the painting was finished, the old master was carried into the studio to pass judgment on the result. His eye rested on a triumph of are. Throwing his arms about the young artist, he exclaimed, "My son, I paint no more."

There are some who shrink from undertaking the work which the Master gives them to do. They are not worthy; they have no skill or power for the delicate duty. But to all their timid shrinking and withdrawing, the Master's gentle yet urgent word is, "Do your best!" They have only to kneel in lowly reverence and pray, for the beloved Master's sake, for skill and strength for the task assigned, and they will be inspired and helped to do it well. The power of Christ will rest upon them and the love of Christ will be in their heart. And all work done under this blessed inspiration will be acceptable unto God. We have but truly to lay the living sacrifice on the altar; then God will send the fire.

We need to get this matter of "consecration" down out of *cloud-land,* into the region of actual, common daily living. We sing about it and pray for it and talk of it in our religious meetings, ofttimes in glowing mood, as if it were some exalted state with which earth's life of toil, struggle, and care had nothing whatever to do. But the consecration suggested by the living sacrifice, is one who walks on the earth, who meets life's actual duties, struggles, temptations, and sorrows, and who does not falter in obedience, fidelity, or submission, but that which follows Christ with love and joy—wherever he leads. No other consecration pleases God.

Chapter 3. Christ's Interest in Our Common Life.

One of our Lord's after-resurrection appearances vividly pictures his loving interest in our common toil. While waiting for him to come to Galilee, the disciples had gone back for a time to their old work of fishing. They were poor men, and this was probably necessary in order to provide for their own subsistence. Thus fishing was the duty that lay nearest to them. Yet it must have been dreary work for them, after the exalted privileges they had enjoyed so long. Think what the last three years had been to these men. Jesus had taken them into the most intimate fellowship with himself—into closest confidential friendship. They had listened to his wonderful *words*, seen his gracious *acts*, and witnessed his sweet life. Think what a privilege it was to live thus with Jesus those beautiful years; what glimpses of heaven they had; what visions of radiant life shone before them.

But now this precious experience was ended. The *lovely dream* had vanished. They were back again at their old work. How dreary it must have been—this tiresome handling of oars and boats and fishing-nets, after their years of exalted life with their Master! But it is a precious thought to us that just at this time, when they were in the midst of the dull and wearisome work, and when they were sadly discouraged, that Christ appeared to them! It showed his interest in their work, his sympathy with them in their discouragement, and his readiness to help them.

The revealings of his appearance that morning, are for all his friends and for all time. We know now that our risen Savior is interested in whatever we have to do, and is ready to help us in all our dull, common life. He will come to his people, not in the church service, the prayer-meeting, the Holy Supper only—but is quite as apt to reveal himself to them in the task-work of the plainest, dullest day.

There are duties in every life, which are irksome. Young people sometimes find school work dull. There are faithful mothers who many a day grow weary of the endless duties of the household. There are good men who tire ofttimes, of the routine of office, or store, or mill, or farm. There comes to most of us, at times, the feeling that what we have to do day after day is not worthy of us. We have had glimpses, or brief experiences, of life in its higher revealings. It may have been a companionship for a season with one above us in experience or attainment, that has lifted us up for a little time into exalted thoughts and feelings, after which it is hard to come back again to the old plodding round, and to the old, uninteresting companionships. It may have been a visit to some place or to some home, with opportunities, refinements, inspirations, privileges, above those which we can have in our own narrower surroundings and plainer home and less congenial intimacies.

Or our circumstances may have been harshly changed by some providence which has broken in upon our happy life. It may have been a *death* which cut off the income; or a reverse in business which swept away a fortune, and luxury and ease and the material refinements and elegances of wealth have to be exchanged for toil and plain circumstances and a humbler home. There are few sorer tests of character, than such changes as these bring with them. The first thought always is: "How can I go to this dreary life, these hard tasks, this painful drudgery, this weary plodding— after having enjoyed so long the comforts and refinements of my old happy state?"

In such cases immeasurable comfort may be found in this appearance of the risen Christ, that morning on the shore. The disciples took up their dull old work because it was necessary, and was their plain duty for the time; and there was Jesus waiting to greet them and bless them. Accept your hard tasks, and do them cheerfully, no matter how irksome they appear—and Christ will reveal himself to you in them. Be sure that he will never come to you when you are avoiding any tasks, when you are withholding your hand from any duty, or when you are fretting and discontented over any circumstances or conditions of your lot. There are no visions of Christ— for *idle dreamers* or for *unhappy shirkers*.

Suppose you have come back, like the disciples, from times of privilege and exaltation, and find yourself face to face once more with an old life which seems now unworthy of you; yet for the time your duty is clear, and if you would have a vision of Christ, you must take up the duty with gladness. Suppose that your home-life is narrow, humdrum, unpoetic, uncongenial, even cold and unkindly; yet there for the time is your place, and there are your duties. And right in this sphere, narrow though it seem, there is room for holiest visions of Christ and for the richest revealings of his grace and blessing!

It will be remembered that Jesus himself, after his glimpse of higher things in the temple, went back to the lowly peasant home at Nazareth, and there for eighteen years more found scope enough for the development of the richest nature this world ever saw, and for the fullest and completest doing of duty ever wrought beneath the skies. Whatever, then, may be our shrinking from dull tasks, our distaste for dreary duty, our discontent with a narrow place and with limiting circumstances, we should go promptly to the work that God assigns, and accept the conditions which lie in the lot which he appoints. And in our hardest toil, our most irksome tasks, our lowliest duties, our dreariest and most uncongenial surroundings, we shall have but to lift up our eyes to see the blessed form of Christ standing before us, with cheer, sympathy, and encouragement for us!

There is more of the lesson. Not only did Christ *reveal* himself to these disciples while at their lowly work—but he *helped* them in it. He told them where to cast their net, and turned their failure to success. We think of Christ as helping us to endure*temptation*, to bear *trial*, to overcome *sin*, to do *spiritual duties*—but we sometimes forget that he is just as ready to help us in our common work. That morning he helped the disciples in their fishing. He will help us in our trade or business, or in whatever work we have to do.

We all have our discouraged days, when things do not go well. The young people fail in their lessons at school, although they have studied hard, and really have done their best. Or the mothers fail in their household work. The children are hard to control. It has been impossible to keep good temper, to maintain that sweetness and lovingness which is so essential to a happy day. They try to be gentle, kindly, and patient—but, try as they will, their minds become ruffled and fretted with cares! They come to the close of the long, unhappy hours disturbed, defeated, discouraged. They have done their best—but they feel that they have only failed. They fall upon their knees—but they have only *tears* for a prayer. Yet if they will lift up their eyes, they will see on the *shore of the troubled sea of their little day's life*—the form of One whose presence will give them strength and confidence, and who will help them to victoriousness. Before his sweet smile, the shadows flee away. At his word, new strength is given, and, after that, work is easy, and all goes well again.

Men, too, in their busy life, are continually called to struggle, ofttimes to suffer. Life is not easy for any who would live godly. Work is hard; burdens are heavy; responsibility is great; trials are sore; duty is large. Life's competitions are fierce; its rivalries are keen; its frictions sometimes grind men's very souls well near to death. It is hard to live sweetly amid the irritations that touch continually at most tender points. It is hard to live lovingly and charitably when they see so much inequity and wrong, and sometimes must themselves endure men's uncharity and injustice. It is hard to toil and never rest, earning even then, scarcely enough to feed and clothe those who are dependent on them for care. *It is hard to meet temptation's fierce assaults, and keep themselves pure, unspotted from the world,* ready for heaven any hour the Lord may come.

It is no wonder that men are sometimes discouraged and lose heart. They are like those weary disciples that spring morning on the Sea of Galilee, after they had toiled all night and had taken nothing. But let us not forget the vision that awaited these disciples with the coming of the dawn—the risen Jesus standing on the shore with his salutation of love and his strong help that instantly turned failure into blessing. So over against every tempted, struggling, toiling life of Christian disciple, Christ is ever standing, ready to give victory and to guide to highest good.

Life would be easier for us—if we could realize the presence and actual help of Christ in all life's experiences. We need to care for only one thing—that we may be faithful always to duty, and loyal to our Master. Then, the duller the round and the sorer the struggle—the surer we shall ever be of Christ's smile and help. We may glory in infirmities, because then the power of God rests upon us.

It is not ordinarily in the easy ways, in the luxurious surroundings, in the paths of worldly honor, in the congenial lot—that the brightest heavenly visions are seen. There have been more blessed revealings of Christ in *prisons* than in *palaces*; in homes of *poverty* than in homes of *abundance*; in ways of *hardship* than in ways of *ease*. We need only to accept our task-work, our drudgery, our toil, in Christ's name—and the glory of Christ will transfigure it and shine upon our faces.

Chapter 4. The Possibilities of Prayer.

We do not begin to realize the possibilities of prayer. There is no limit, for example, to the *scope* of prayer. We may embrace in it all things that belong to our life—not merely those which affect our *spiritual* interests—but those as well which seem to be only *temporal* matters. Nothing which concerns us in any way—is matter of indifference to God. One writes: "Learn to entwine with your prayers—the small cares, the trifling sorrows, the little needs of daily life. Whatever affects you—be it a changed look, an altered tone, an unkind word, a wrong, a wound, a demand you cannot meet, a sorrow you cannot disclose—turn it into prayer and send it up to God! Disclosures you may not make to man—you can make to the Lord. Men may be too little for your great matters; God is not too great for your small ones. Only give yourself to prayer, whatever be the occasion that calls for it."

We soon find, however, if we are really earnest, that our desires are too great for words. We have in our hearts feelings, hungerings, affections, longings, which we want to breathe out to God; but when we begin to speak to him, we find no language adequate for their expression. We try to tell God of our sorrow for sin, of our weakness and sinfulness; of our desire to be better, to love Christ more, to follow him more closely, and of our hunger after righteousness, after holiness; but it is very little of these deep cravings that we can get into speech.

Language is a wonderful gift. The power of putting into words the thoughts and emotions of our souls, that others may understand them, is one of the most marvelous powers the Creator has bestowed upon us. Thus we communicate our feelings and desires, from one to the other. It is a sore deprivation when the gates of speech are shut and locked, and when the soul cannot tell its thoughts.

Yet we all know, unless our thoughts and feelings are very shallow and trivial, that even the wonderful faculty of language is inadequate to express all that the soul can experience. No true orator ever finds sentences majestic enough to interpret the sentiments that burn in his soul. Deep, pure love is never able to put into words its most sacred feelings and emotions. It is only the commonplace of the inner life that can be uttered in even the finest language. There is always more that lies back, unexpressed, than is spoken in any words.

It is specially true of prayer—that we cannot utter its deepest feelings and holiest desires. We have comfort, however, in the assurance that God can hear thoughts. He knows what we want to say and cannot express. Your dearest friend may stand close to you when your mind is full of thoughts—but unless you speak or give some sign, he cannot know one of your thoughts. He may lay his ear close to your heart, and he will hear its throbbings; but he cannot hear your feelings, your desires. Yet God knows all that goes on in your soul. Every thought which flies through your brain, is heard in heaven.

"O Lord, you have examined my heart and know everything about me. You know when I sit down or stand up. You know my every thought when far away. You chart the path ahead of me and tell me where to stop and rest. Every moment you know where I am. You know what I am going to say even before I say it, Lord." Psalm 139:1-4

We need not trouble ourselves, therefore, if we cannot get our wishes into words when we pray, for God hears wishes, heart-longings, soul hungerings and thirstings. The things we cannot say in speech of the lips, we may ask God to take from our heart's speech. There is not the feeblest, faintest glimmer of a desire rising on the far-away horizon of our being—but God sees it. There is not a heart-hunger, not a wish to be holier and better, not an aspiration to be more Christ-like, not a craving to live for God and be a blessing to others, not the faintest desire to be rid of sin's power—but God knows of it. Paul has a wonderful word on this subject: God, he says, "is able to do exceeding abundantly above all that we ask or think." When our heart is stirred to its depths, what large, great things can we ask in words? Then, how much can we put into thoughts of prayer, into longings, desires, aspirations, beyond the possibilities of speech? God can do more than we can pray, either in words or thoughts.

Our truest praying is that which we cannot express in any words, our heart's unutterable longings, when we sit at God's feet and look up into his face and do not speak at all—but let our hearts talk.

Our best, truest prayers are not for earthly things—but for spiritual blessings. When the objects are temporal, we do not know what we should pray for—what would be really a blessing to us. You are a loving parent, and your child is very ill. It seems that it must die. You fall upon your knees before God to pray—but you do not know what to ask. Your breaking heart would quickly plead, "Lord, spare my precious child"; but you do not know that that is best. Perhaps to live would not be God's sweetest gift to your child, or to you. So, not daring to choose, you can only say, "Lord God, I cannot speak more; but you know your child; you understand what is best."

Or, some plan of yours, which you have long cherished, seems about to be thwarted. You go to God, and begin to pray; but you do not know what to ask. You can only say, "Lord, I cannot tell what is best; but you know." What a comfort it is that God does indeed know, and that we may safely leave our heart's burden in his hand, without any request whatever!

We can do little more than this, in any request for temporal things. Says Farrar: "There are two things to remember about prayers for earthly things: One, that to ask mainly for earthly blessings is a dreadful dwarfing and vulgarization of the grandeur of prayer, as though you asked for a handful of grass, when you might ask for a handful of emeralds; the other that you must always ask for earthly desires with absolute submission of your own will to God's." So silence is oft-times the best and truest praying—bowing before God in life's great crises; but saying nothing, leaving the burden in God's hand without any of your own choosing. We are always safe when we let God guide us in all our ways.

Many of the richest possibilities of prayer, lie beyond valleys of pain and sorrow. The best things of life cannot be gotten, but at sore cost. When we pray for more holiness, we do not know what we are asking for; at least we do not know the price we must pay to get that which we ask. Our "Nearer, my God, to Thee," must be conditioned by, and often can come only through, "Even though it be a cross—that raises me."

Not only are the spiritual things the best things—but many times the spiritual things can be grasped only by letting go and losing out of our hands those earthly things we would love to keep. God loves us too much to grant our prayers for comfort and relief—if he can do it only at spiritual loss to us. He would rather let it be hard for us to live if there is blessing in the hardness, than make it easy for us at the cost of the blessing.

There are certain singing-birds that never learn to sing—until their cages are darkened. Would it be true kindness to keep these birds always in the sunshine? There are human hearts that never learn to sing the song of faith and peace and love—until they enter the darkness of trial. Would it be true love for these if God would hear their prayers for the removal of their pain? We dare not plead, therefore, but with utmost self-distrust and submission, that God would remove the cross of suffering.

Does God answer prayers? "I have been praying for one thing for years," says one, "and it has not come yet." God has many ways of answering. Sometimes he *delays* that he may give a better, fuller answer. A poor woman stood at a vineyard gate, and looked over into the vineyard. "Would you like some grapes?" asked the proprietor, who was within. "I would be very thankful," replied the woman. "Then bring your basket." Quickly the basket was brought to the gate and passed in. The owner took it and was gone a long time among the vines, until the woman became discouraged, thinking he was not coming again. At last he returned with the basket heaped full. "I have made you wait a good while," he said, "but you know the longer you have to wait, the better grapes and the more."

So it sometimes is in prayer. We bring our empty vessel to God—and pass it over the gate of prayer to him. He seems to be delaying a long time, and sometimes faith faints with waiting. But at last he comes, and our basket is heaped full with luscious blessings! He waited long that he might bring us a better and a fuller answer. At least we are sure that no true prayer ever really goes unanswered. We have to *wait* for the fruits to ripen—and that takes time! Sometimes God delays—until some work in us is finished.

Chapter 5. Getting Christ's Touch.

There was wonderful power in the *touch of Christ,* when he was on the earth. Wherever he laid his hand, he left a blessing—and sick, sad, and weary ones received health, comfort, and peace. That hand, glorified, now holds in its clasp the seven stars. Yet there are senses in which the blessed touch of Christ is felt yet on men's lives. He is as really in this world today, as he was when he walked in human form through Judea and Galilee. His hand is yet laid on his weary, suffering, sorrowing people, and, though its pressure is unfelt, its power to bless is the same as in the ancient days. It is laid on the sick, when precious heavenly words of cheer and encouragement from the Scriptures are read at their bedside, giving them the blessing of sweet patience, and quieting their fears. It is laid on the sorrowing, when the consolations of divine love come to their hearts with tender comfort, giving them strength to submit to God's will and rejoice in the midst of trial. It is laid on the faint and weary, when the grace of Christ comes to them with its holy peace, hushing the wild tumult, and giving true rest of soul.

But there is another way in which the hand of Christ is laid on human lives. He sends his disciples into the world to represent him. "As the Father has sent me, even so I send you," is his own word. Of course the best and holiest Christian life—can be only the dimmest, faintest reproduction of the rich, full, blessed life of Christ. Yet it is in this way, through these earthen vessels, that he has ordained to save the world, and to heal, help, comfort, lift up, and build up men.

Perhaps in thinking of what God does for the world, we are too apt to overlook the human agents and instruments, and to think of him touching lives directly and immediately. A friend of ours is in sorrow, and, going to our knees, we pray to God to give him comfort. But may it not be that he would send the comfort through *our* own heart and lips? One we love is not doing well, is drifting away from a true life, is in danger of being lost. In anguish of heart we cry to God, beseeching him to lay his hand on the imperilled life, and rescue it. But may it not be that *ours* is the hand that must be stretched out in love, and laid, in Christ's name, on the life that is in danger?

Certain it is, at least, that each one of us who knows the love of Christ, is ordained to be *as Christ* to others; that is, to be the messenger to carry to them the gift of Christ's grace and help, and to show to them the spirit of Christ, the patience, gentleness, thoughtfulness, love, and yearning of Christ. We are taught to say, "Christ lives in me." If this is true, Christ would love others through us, and our touch must be to others as the very touch of Christ himself. Every Christian ought to be, in his measure, a new incarnation of the Christ, so that people shall say: "He interprets Christ to me! He comforts me in my sorrow—as Christ himself would do if he were to come and sit down beside me! He is as hopeful and patient as Christ would be—if he were to return and take me as his disciple."

But before we can be in the place of Christ to sorrowing, suffering, and struggling ones—we must have that mind in us, which was in him. When Paul said, "The love of Christ constrains me," he meant that he had the very love of Christ in him—the love which loved even the most unlovely, which helped even the most unworthy, which was gentle and affectionate even to the most loathsome. We are never ready to do good in the world, in the truest sense or in any large measure—until we have become thus filled with the very spirit of Christ! We may help people in a certain way, without loving them. We may render them services of a certain kind, benefitting them externally or temporally. We may put material gifts into their hands, build them houses, purchase clothing for them, carry them bread, or improve their circumstances and condition. We may thus do many things for them—without having in our heart any love for them. This is nothing better than common philanthropy. But the highest and most real help we can give them, only through sincerely loving them.

"When I have attempted," says Emerson, "to give myself to others by services, it proved an intellectual trick—no more. They eat your services like apples, and leave you out. But love them, and they feel you and delight in you all the time." When we love others, we can help them in all deep and true ways. We can put blessings into their hearts instead of merely into their hands. We can enter into their very being, becoming new breath of life to them—quickening and inspiring them.

There is a touching and very suggestive story of a good woman in Sweden, who opened a home for crippled and diseased children—children for whom no one else was ready to care. In due time she received into her home about twenty of these unfortunate little ones. Among them was a boy of three years, who was a most frightful and disagreeable object. He resembled a skeleton. His skin was covered with hideous blotches and sores. He was always whining and crying. This poor little fellow gave the good lady more care and trouble than all the others together. She did her best for him, and was as kind as possible—washed him, fed him, nursed him. But the child was so repulsive in his looks and ways, that, try as she would, she could not bring herself to like him, and often her disgust would show itself in her face in spite of her effort to hide it. She could not really love the child.

One day she was sitting on the veranda steps with this child in her arms. The sun was shining brightly, and the perfume of the autumn honeysuckles, the chirping of the birds, and the buzzing of the insects, lulled her into a sort of sleep. Then in a half-waking, half-dreaming state, she thought of herself as having changed places with the child, and as lying there, only more foul, more repulsive in her sinfulness than he was.

Over her she saw the Lord Jesus bending, looking lovingly into her face, yet with an expression of gentle rebuke in his eye, as if he meant to say, "If I can bear with you who are so full of sin, surely you ought, for my sake, to love that innocent child who suffers for the sin of his parents."

She woke up with a sudden startle, and looked into the boy's face. He had waked, too, and was looking very earnestly into her face. Sorry for her past disgust, and feeling in her heart a new compassion for him, she bent her face to his, and kissed him as tenderly as ever she had kissed a babe of her own. With a startled look in his eyes, and a flush on his cheek, the boy gave her back a smile so sweet that she had never seen one like it before. From that moment a wonderful change came over the child. He understood the new affection that had come—instead of dislike and loathing in the woman's heart. That touch of human love transformed his peevish, fretful nature into gentle quiet and beauty. The woman had seen a vision of herself in that blotched, repulsive child, and of Christ's wonderful love for her in spite of her sinfulness. Under the inspiration of this vision she had become indeed *as Christ* to the child. The love of Christ had come into her heart, and was pouring through her upon that poor, wretched, wronged life.

Christ loves the unlovely, the deformed, the loathsome, the leprous. We have only to think of ourselves as we are in his sight, and then remember that, in spite of all the moral and spiritual loathsomeness in us—he yet loves us, does not shrink from us, lays his hand upon us to heal us, takes us into most intimate companionship with himself. This Christian woman had seen a vision of herself, and of Christ loving her still and condescending to bless and save her; and now she was ready to be *as Christ*, to show the spirit of Christ, to be the pity and the love of Christ to this poor, loathsome child lying on her knee.

She had gotten the *touch of Christ* by getting the *love of Christ* into her heart. And we can get it in no other way. We must see ourselves as Christ's servants, sent by him to be to others—what he is to us. Then shall we be fitted to be a blessing to every life which our life touches. Our words then shall throb with love, and find their way to the hearts of the weary and sorrowing. Then there will be a *sympathetic* quality in our life, which shall give a strange power of helpfulness to whatever we do.

Says a thoughtful writer, speaking of influence: "Let a man press nearer to Christ, and open his nature more widely to admit the power of Christ, and, whether he knows it or not—it is better, perhaps, if he does not know it—he will certainly be growing in power for God with men, and for men with God." We get *power* for Christ—only as we become filled with the very *life* of Christ!

Everywhere about us—there are lives, cold, and cheerless, and dull, which by the touch of our hand, in loving warmth, in Christ's name, would be wondrously blessed and transformed. Someone tells of going into a jeweler's store to look at certain gems. Among other stones he was shown an opal. As it lay there, however, it appeared dull and altogether lustreless. Then the jeweler took it in his hand and held it for some moments, and again showed it to his customer. Now it gleamed and flashed with all the glories of the rainbow. It needed the touch and warmth of a human hand to bring out its iridescence. There are human lives everywhere about us that are rich in their possibilities of beauty and glory. No gems or jewels are so precious; but as we see them in their earthly condition they are dull and lustreless, without brightness or loveliness. Perhaps they are even covered with stain by sin. Yet they need only the touch of the hand of Christ—to bring out the radiance, the loveliness, the beauty of the divine image in them. And you and I must be the hand of Christ to these lusterless or stained lives! Touching them with our warm love, the sleeping splendor which is in them, hidden perhaps under sin's marring and ruin, will yet shine out—the beginning of glory for them!

Chapter 6. The Blessing of a Burden.

It is not always the *easiest* things—which are the *best* things. Usually we have to pay a high price, for any good thing. In all markets, commodities which *cost* little may be set down as *worth* but little. All our blessings may be rated in the same way. If they come easily, without great cost of effort or sacrifice, their value to us is not great. But if we can get them only through self-denial, tears, anguish, and pain—we may be sure that they hide in them the very *gold of God*. So it is that many of our best and richest blessings come to us in some form of *rugged hardness*.

Take what we call **drudgery**. Life is full of it. It begins in childhood. There is school, with its set hours, its lessons, rules, tables, tasks, recitations. Then, when we grow up, instead of getting away from this bondage of routine, this interminable drudgery, it goes on just as in childhood. It is rising at the same hour every morning, and hurrying away to the day's tasks, and doing the same things over and over, six days in the week, fifty-two weeks in the year, and on and on unto life's end. For the great majority of us, there is almost no break in the monotonous rounds of our days through the long years. Many of us sigh and wish we might in some way free ourselves from this endless routine. We think of it as a sore bondage and by no means the ideal of a noble and beautiful life.

But really, much that is best in life comes out of this very bondage to drudgery. A recent writer suggests a new beatitude: "Blessed be drudgery." He reminds us that no Bible beatitude comes easily—but that every one of them is the fruit of some experience of hardness or pain. He shows us that life's drudgery, wearisome and disagreeable as it is, yields rich treasures of good and blessing. Drudgery, he tells us, is the secret of all culture. He names as fundamentals in a strong, fine character, "power of attention; power of industry; promptitude in beginning work; method, accuracy, and adroitness in doing work; perseverance; courage before difficulties; cheer under straining burdens; self-control; self-denial; temperance"; and claims that nowhere else can these qualities be gotten—but in the unending grind and pressure of those routine duties which we call *drudgery*. "It is because we have to go, morning after morning, through rain, through shine, through headache, heartache—to the appointed spot and do the appointed work; because, and only because, we have to stick to that work through the eight or ten hours, long after rest would be so sweet; because the school-boy's lessons must be learned at nine o'clock, and learned without a slip; because the accounts on the ledger must square to a cent; because the goods must tally exactly with the invoice; because good temper must be kept with children, customers, neighbors, not seven times—but seventy times seven; because the besetting sin must be watched today, tomorrow, next day; in short—it is because, and only because, of the rut, plod, grind, hum-drum in the work—that we get at last those self-foundations laid," which are essential to all noble character.

So there is a blessing for us in the commonest, wearisomest task-work of our lives. "Blessed be drudgery" is truly a beatitude. We all need the discipline of this tireless plodding, to build us up into beautiful character. Even the loveliest flowers must have their roots in *common earth*; so, many of the sweetest things in human lives grow out of the *soil of drudgery*. "Be O man, like unto the rose. Its root is indeed in dirt and mud—but its flowers still send forth grace and perfume."

Take again life's **struggles** and **conflicts**. There are, in the experience of each one, obstacles, hindrances, and difficulties, which make it hard to live successfully. Everyone has to move onward and upward through ranks of resistances. This is true of physical life. Every baby that is born, begins at once a struggle for existence. To be victorious and live—or to succumb and die? is the question of every cradle, and only half the babies born reach their teens. After that, until its close, life is a continuous struggle with the manifold forms of physical infirmity. If we live to be old, it must be through our victoriousness over the unceasing antagonism of *accident* and *disease*.

The same is true in *mental* progress. It must be made against resistance. It is never easy to become a scholar or to attain intellectual culture. It takes years and years of study and discipline to draw out and train the faculties of the mind. An indolent, self-indulgent student may have an easy time; he never troubles himself with difficult problems; he lets the hard things pass, not vexing his brain with them. But in evading the burden—he misses the blessing that was in it for him. The only path to the joys and rewards of scholarship is that of patient, persistent toil.

It is true also in *spiritual* life. We enter a world of antagonism and opposition the moment we resolve at Christ's feet, to be Christians, to be true men or women, to forsake sin, to obey God, to do our duty. There never comes a day when we can live nobly and worthily without effort, without resistance to wrong influences, without struggle against the power of temptation. It never gets easy to be godly. Evermore the cross lies at our feet, and daily it must be taken up and carried, if we would follow Christ. We are apt to grow weary of this unending struggle, and to become discouraged, because there is neither rest nor abatement in it.

But here again we learn that it is out of just such struggles that we must get the nobleness and beauty of character, after which we are striving. This is the universal law of spiritual growth. There must be resistance, struggle, conflict—or there can be no development of strength. We are inclined to pity those whose lives are scenes of toil and hardship—but God does not pity them, if only they are victorious; for in their overcoming they are climbing daily upward toward the holy heights of sainthood. The beatitudes in the Apocalypse are all for *over-comers*. Heaven's rewards and crowns lie beyond battle-plains. Spiritual life always needs *opposition*. It flourishes most luxuriantly in *adverse* circumstances. We grow best under afflictions. We find our richest blessings—in the burdens we dread to take up.

The word "character" in its origin is suggestive. It is from a root which signifies to engrave, to cut into furrows. In life, therefore, it is that which experiences cut or furrow in the soul. A baby has no character. Its life is like a piece of white paper, with nothing yet written upon it; or it is like a smooth marble tablet, on which, as yet, the sculptor has cut nothing; or the canvas, waiting for the painter's colors. Character is formed as the years go on. It is the writing—the song, the story, put upon the paper. It is the engraving, the sculpturing, which the marble receives under the chisel. It is the picture which the artist paints on the canvas. Final character is what a man is, when he has lived through all his earthly years. In the Christian it is the lines of the likeness of Christ engraved, sometimes furrowed and scarred, upon his soul by the divine Spirit through the means of grace and the experiences of his own life.

I saw a beautiful vase, and asked its story. Once it was a lump of common clay lying in the darkness. Then it was harshly dug out and crushed and ground in the mill, and then put upon the wheel and shaped, then polished and tinted and put into the furnace and burned. At last, after many processes, it stood upon the table—a gem of graceful beauty. In some way analogous to this, every noble character is formed. Common clay at first, it passes through a thousand processes and experiences, many of them hard and painful, until at length it is presented before God, faultless in its beauty, bearing the features of Christ himself.

Spiritual beauty never can be reached without cost. The *blessing* is always hidden away in the *burden*, and can be gotten only by lifting the burden. Self must die if the good in us is to live and shine out in radiance. Michael Angelo used to say, as the chippings flew thick from the marble on the floor of his studio, "While the marble wastes, the image grows." There must be a wasting of self, a chipping away continually of things that are dear to nature, if the things that are true, and just, and honorable, and pure, and lovely, are to come out in the life. The marble must waste, while the image grows.

Then take *suffering*. Here, too, the same law prevails. Everyone suffers. Said Augustine, "God had one Son without sin—but none without sorrow." From infancy's first cry until the old man's life goes out in a gasp of pain, suffering is a condition of existence. It comes in manifold forms. Now it is in sickness; the body is racked with pain or burns in fever. Ofttimes sickness is a heavy burden. Yet even this burden has a blessing in it for the Christian. Sickness rightly borne, makes us better. It unbinds the world's fetters. It purifies the heart. It sobers the spirit. It turns the eyes heavenward. It strips off much of the *illusion of life* and uncovers its better realities. Sickness in a home of faith, prayer, and love, softens all the household hearts, makes sympathy deeper, and draws all the family closer together.

Trouble comes in many other forms. It may be a bitter *disappointment* which falls upon a young life when love has not been true, or when character has proved unworthy, turning the fair blossoms of hope, to dead leaves under the feet. There are lives that bear the pain and carry the hidden memorials of such a grief through long years, making them sad at heart even when walking in sweetest sunshine.

Or it may be the *failure* of some other hope, as when one has followed a bright dream of ambition for days and years, finding it only a dream. Or it may be the keener, more bitter grief which comes to one when a friend—a child, a brother or sister, a husband or wife—fails badly. In such a case even the divine comfort cannot heal the heart's hurt; love cannot but suffer, and there is no hand that can lessen the pang. The anguish which love endures for others' sins is among the saddest of earth's sorrows.

There are griefs which wear no black garments, which close no shutters, which drop no tears which men can see, which can get no sympathy—but that of the blessed Christ and perhaps of a closest human brother, and must wear smiles before men and go on with life's work as if all were gladness within the heart. If we knew the inner life of many of the people we meet, we would be very gentle with them and would excuse the things in them that seem strange or eccentric to us. They are carrying burdens of secret grief. We cannot begin to know the sorrows of others.

There is no need to try to solve that old, yet always new, question of human hearts, "Why does God permit so much suffering in his children?" It is idle to ask this question, and all efforts at answering it are not only vain—but they are even irreverent. We may be sure, however, of one thing, that in *every pain and trial, there is a blessing folded*. We may miss it—but it is there, and the loss is ours if we do not get it. Every night of sorrow carries in its dark bosom, its own lamps of comfort. The darkness of grief and trial is full of benedictions.

The most blessed lives in the world are those that have borne the burden of suffering. "Where, think you," asks James Martineau, "does the Heavenly Father hear the tones of deepest love, and see on the uplifted face the light of most heartfelt gratitude? Not where his gifts are most profuse—but where they are most meager; not within the halls of successful ambition, or even in the dwellings of unbroken domestic peace; but where the outcast, flying from persecution, kneels in the evening on the rocks whereon he sleeps; at the fresh grave, where, as the earth is opened, heaven in answer opens too; by the pillow of the wasted sufferer, where the sunken eye, denied sleep, converses with the silent stars, and the hollow voice enumerates in low prayer the scanty list of comforts, the easily remembered blessings, and the shortened tale of hopes. Genial, almost to a miracle, is the soil of sorrow, wherein the smallest seed of love, timely falling, becomes a tree, in whose foliage the birds of blessed song lodge and sing unceasingly."

The truly happiest, sweetest, tenderest homes are not those where there has been no sorrow—but those which have been overshadowed with grief, and where Christ's comfort was accepted. The very memory of the sorrow is a gentle benediction that broods ever over the household, like the afterglow of sunset, like the silence that comes after prayer.

In every burden of sorrow, there is a blessing sent from God, which we ought not to thrust away. In one of the battles of the Crimea, a cannon-ball gashed the earth and sadly marring the garden beauty of the place. But from the ugly chasm there burst forth a spring of water, which flowed on thereafter, a living fountain. So the strokes of sorrow gash our hearts, leaving ofttimes wounds and scars—but they open for us fountains of rich blessing and of new life.

These are hints of the *blessings of burdens*. Our dull task-work, accepted, will train us into strong and noble character. Our temptations and hardships, met victoriously, knit muscles and sinews of strength in our souls. Our pain and sorrow, endured with sweet trust and submission, leave us with life purified and enriched, with more of Christ in us. In every *burden* that God lays upon us, there is a *blessing* for us, if only we will take it.

Chapter 7. Heart-peace Before Ministry.

Peace in the heart is one of the conditions of good work. We cannot do our best in anything if we are fretted and anxious. A feverish heart makes an inflamed brain, a clouded eye, and an unsteady hand. The people who really accomplish the most, and achieve the best results, are those of calm, self-controlled spirit. Those who are nervous and excited may be always busy, and always under pressure of haste; but in the end they do far less work than if they wrought calmly and steadily, and were never in a hurry.

Nervous haste is always hindering haste. It does faulty work, and does but little of it in the end. Really rapid workers are always deliberate in their movements, never appearing to be in any hurry whatever; and yet they pass swiftly from task to task, doing each duty well because they are calm and unflustered, and, with their wits about them, work with clear eye, steady nerve, and skillful hand.

An eminent French surgeon used to say to his students, when they were engaged in difficult and delicate operations, in which coolness and firmness were needed, "Gentlemen, don't be in a hurry; for there's no time to lose."

The people in all lines of duty who do the most work are the calmest, most unhurried people in the community. Duties never wildly chase each other in their lives. One task never crowds another out, nor ever compels hurried, and therefore imperfect, doing. The calm spirit works methodically, doing one thing at a time, and doing it well; and it therefore works swiftly, though never appearing to be in haste.

We need the peace of God in our heart, just as really for the doing well of the little things of our secular life—as for the doing of the greatest duties of Christ's kingdom. Our face ought to shine, and our spirit ought to be tranquil, and our eye ought to be clear, and our nerves ought to be steady, as we press through the tasks of our commonest day. Then we shall do them all well, slurring nothing, marring nothing. We need heart-peace before we begin any day's duties, and we should wait at Christ's feet until we get his quieting touch upon our heart before we go forth.

It is especially true in spiritual work that we must know the secret of peace before we can minister either swiftly or effectively to others in our Master's name. Feverishness of spirit makes the hand unskillful in delicate duty. A troubled heart cannot give comfort to other troubled hearts; it must first become calm and quiet. It is often said that one who has suffered is prepared to help others in suffering; but this is true only when one has suffered victoriously, and has passed up out of the deep, dark valley of pain and tears—to the radiant mountain-tops of peace. An uncomforted mourner cannot be a messenger of consolation to another in grief. One whose heart is still vexed and uncalmed, cannot be a physician to hearts with bleeding wounds. We must first have been comforted by God ourselves, before we can comfort others in their tribulations.

The same is true of all spiritual ministry. We need a steady hand to work faithfully in Christ's kingdom. One of our Lord's earlier miracles furnishes an illustration of this truth. Jesus was called to heal a woman who lay sick with a great fever. One of the Gospels describes the cure in these striking words: "He touched her hand, and the fever left her; and she arose and ministered unto them." We readily understand this record in its primary reference to the physical cure that was wrought by our Lord. We know, of course, that the woman could not minister to others while the fever was on her. When sore sickness comes, the busiest, fullest hands must drop their tasks. No matter how important the work is, how essential it may appear, it must be laid down when painful illness seizes us. We must be healed of our fever, before we can minister.

But there are other fevers besides those which burn in men's bodies. There are heart-fevers which may rage within us, even when our bodies are in perfect health. We find people with feverish spirits—unhappy, discontented, fretted, worried, perhaps unsubmissive and rebellious. Or they may be in a fever of fear or dread. These inward fevers are worse evils than mere bodily illness. It is better in sickness to have our heart's fever depart, even though we must longer keep our pain, than to recover our physical health, meanwhile keeping our fretfulness and impatience uncured.

We cannot minister while heart-fever of any kind is on us. We may go on with our work—but we cannot do it well, and there will be little blessing in it. Discontent hinders any life's usefulness. Jesus loved Martha, and accepted her service because he knew she loved him; but he plainly told her that her feverishness was not beautiful, and that it detracted from the worth and the full acceptableness of the good work she did; and he pointed her to Mary's quiet peace as a better way of living and serving. Anxiety of any kind, unfits us in some degree for work. It is only when Christ comes and lays his hand upon our heart, and cures its fever, that we are ready for ministering in his name, in the most efficient way.

There is a little story of a busy woman's life which illustrates this lesson. She was the mother of a large family, and, sometimes, in the multiplicity of her tasks and cares, she lost the sweetness of her peace, and, like Martha, became troubled and worried with her much serving. One morning she had been unusually hurried, and things had not gone smoothly. She had breakfast to get for her family, her husband to care for as he hastened away early to his work, and her children to make ready for school. There were other household duties which filled the poor, weak woman's hands, until her strength was well-near utterly exhausted. And she had not gone through it all that morning in a sweet, peaceful way. She had allowed herself to lose her patience, and to grow fretful, vexed, and unhappy. She had spoken quick, hasty, petulant words to her husband and her children. Her heart had been in a fever of irritation and disquiet all the morning.

When the children were gone, and the pressing tasks were finished, and the house was all quiet, the tired woman crept upstairs to her own room. She was greatly discouraged. She felt that her morning had been a most unsatisfactory one; that she had sadly failed in her duty; that she had grieved her Master by her lack of patience and gentleness, and had hurt her children's lives by her fretfulness and her ill-tempered words. Shutting her door, she took up her Bible and read the story of the healing of the sick woman: "He touched her hand, and the fever left her; and she arose and ministered unto them."

"Ah!" said she, "if I could have had that touch before I began my morning's work, the fever would have left me, and I should have been prepared to minister sweetly and peacefully to my family." She had learned that she needed the touch of Christ to make her ready for beautiful and gentle service.

In contrast with this story, and showing the blessed sweetness and holy influence of a life that gets Christ's touch in the morning, there is this account by Farrar of his mother: "My mother's habit was, every day, immediately after breakfast, to withdraw for an hour to her own room, and to spend that hour in reading the Bible, in meditation, and in prayer. From that hour, as from a pure fountain, she drew the strength and the sweetness which enabled her to fulfill all her duties, and to remain unruffled by all the worries and pettinesses which are so often the intolerable trial of poor neighborhoods. As I think of her life, and of all it had to bear, I see the absolute triumph of Christian grace in the lovely ideal of a Christian lady. I never saw her temper disturbed; I never heard her speak one word of anger, or of calumny, or of idle gossip. I never observed in her any sign of a single sentiment unbecoming to a soul which had drunk of the river of the water of life, and which had fed upon *manna* in the barren wilderness."

There are many busy mothers to whom this lesson may come almost as a revelation. No hands are fuller of tasks, no heart is fuller of cares, than the hands and the heart of a mother of a large family of young children. It is little wonder if sometimes she loses her sweetness of spirit in the pressure of care that is upon her. But this lesson is worth learning. Let the mothers wait on their knees each morning, before they begin their work, for the touch of Christ's hand upon their heart. Then the fever will leave them, and they can enter with calm peace on the work of the long, hard day.

The lesson, however, is for us all. We are in no condition for godly work of any kind, when we are fretted and anxious in mind. It is only when the peace of God is in our heart that we are ready for true and really helpful ministry. A feverish heart makes a worried face, and a worried face casts a shadow. A troubled spirit mars the temper and disposition. It unfits one for being a comforter of others, for giving cheer and inspiration, for touching other lives with godly and helpful impulses. *Peace* must come before *ministry*. We need to have our fever cured before we go out to our work. Hence, we should begin each new day at the Master's feet, and get his cooling, quieting touch upon our hot hand. Then, and not until then, shall we be ready for godly service in his name.

Chapter 8. Moral Curvatures.

Our Lord's miracles are parables in act. A woman came to him bent almost double, and went away straight. The human form is made for erectness. This is one of the marks of nobility in man, in contrast with the downward bending and looking of other animals. Man is the only creature that bears this erect form. It is a part of the image of God upon him. It indicates heavenly aspiration, hunger for God, desire for pure and lofty things, capacity for immortal blessedness. It tells of man's hope and home above the earth, beyond the stars. Says an old writer, "God gave to man a face directed upwards, and bade him look at the heavens, and raise his uplifted countenance toward the stars." The Greek word for "man" meant the upward looking. The bending of the form and face downward, toward the earth, has always been the symbol of a soul turned unworthily toward lower things, forgetful of its true home.

The look of a man's eyes, tells where his heart is, where his desires are reaching and tending, how his life is growing.

There are a great many *bent people* in the world. Physical bending may be caused by accident or disease, and is no mark of spiritual curvature. Many a deformed body is the home of a noble and holy soul, with eyes and aspirations turned upward toward God. I remember a woman in my first parish who then for fourteen years had sat in her chair, unable to lift hand or foot, every joint drawn, her wasted body frightfully bent. Yet she had a transfigured face, telling of a beautiful soul within. Joy and peace shone out through that poor tortured body. Disease may drag down the erect form, until all its beauty is gone, and the inner life meanwhile may be erect as an angel, with its eyes and aspirations turned upward toward God.

But there are crooked souls—souls that are bent down. This may be the case even while the body is straight as an arrow. There are men and women whose forms are admired for their erectness, their attractive proportions, their graceful movements, their lovely features, yet whose souls are debased, whose desires are groveling, whose characters are sadly misshapen and deformed.

Sin always bends the soul. Many a young man comes out from a holy home in the beauty and strength of youth, wearing the unsullied robes of innocence, with eye clear and uplifted, with aspirations for noble things, with hopes that are exalted; but a few years later he appears a debased and ruined man, with soul bent sadly downward. The bending begins in slight yieldings to sin—but the tendency unchecked, grows and fixes itself in the life in permanent moral disfigurement.

A stage-driver had held the lines for many years, and when he grew old, his hands were bent, and his fingers were so stiffened that they could not be straightened out. There is a similar process that goes on in men's souls when they continue to do the same things over and over. One who is trained from childhood to be gentle, kindly, patient, to control the temper, to speak softly, to be loving and charitable—will grow into the radiant beauty of love. One who accustoms himself to think habitually and only of noble and worthy things, who sets his affections on things above, and strives to reach "whatever things are true, whatever things are honest, whatever things are pure, whatever things are lovely," will grow continually upward, toward spiritual beauty. But on the other hand, if one gives way from childhood to all ugly tempers, all resentful feelings, all bitterness and anger, his life will shape itself into the unbeauty of these dispositions. One whose mind turns to debasing things, things unholy, unclean—will find his whole soul bending and growing toward the earth in permanent *moral curvature.*

There is also a bending of the life by *sorrow.* The experience of sorrow is scarcely less perilous than that of temptation. The common belief is that grief always makes people better. But this is not true. If the sufferer submits to God with loving confidence, and is victorious through faith, sorrow's outcome is blessing and good. But many are crushed by their sorrow. They yield to it, and it bears them down beneath its weight. They turn their faces away from the light of God, toward the grave's darkness, and their souls grow toward the gloom.

Here is a mother who several years since lost by death a beautiful daughter. The mother was a Christian woman, and her child was also a Christian, dying in sweet hope. Yet never since that coffin was closed has the mother lifted up her eyes toward God in submission and hope. She visits the cemetery on Sundays—but never the church. She goes with downcast look about her home, weeping whenever her daughter's name is mentioned, and complains of God's hardness and unkindness in taking away her child. She is bent down with her eyes to the earth, and sees only the clods and the dust and the grave's gloom—and sees not the blue sky, the bright stars, and the sweet face of the Father. So long has she now been thus bowed down in the habit of sadness and grieving, that she can in no way lift herself up.

Since I began to write this chapter I have had a long talk with one whose life is sorely bent. Ten years since I first knew her as a bright and happy young girl, her face sunny in the light of God's love. Trouble came into her life in many forms. Her own father proved unworthy, failing in all the sacred duties of affection toward his child. Events in her own life were disappointing and discouraging. Friends in whom she had trusted failed in that faithfulness and helpfulness which one has a right to expect from one's friends. There was a succession of unhappy experiences, through several years, all tending to hurt her heart-life. As the result of all this, she has become embittered and hardened, not only against those who have wronged her and treated her unjustly—but even against God. So long has she yielded to these feelings that her whole life has been bent down from its upward, Godward look, into settled despondency. God has altogether faded out of her soul's vision, and she thinks of him only as unkind and unjust. To restore her life to its former brightness and beauty will require a moral miracle as great as that by which the body of the crooked woman was made straight.

Then there are lives also that are bowed down by toil and care. For many people, life's burdens are very heavy. There are fathers of large families who sometimes find their load almost more than they can bear, in their efforts to provide for those who are dear to them. There are mothers who, under their burdens of household care, at times feel themselves bowed down, and scarcely able longer to go on. In all places of responsibility, where men are called to stand, the load many times grows very heavy, and stalwart forms bend under it. *This world's work is hard for most of us.* Life is not play—to any who take it earnestly.

And many people yield to the weight of a *duty*, and let themselves be bent down under it. We see men bowing under their load, until their very body grows crooked, and they can look only downward. We see them become prematurely old. The light goes out of their eyes; the freshness fades out of their cheeks; the sweetness leaves their spirit. Few things in life are sadder than the way some people let themselves be bent down by their load of duty or care. There really is no reason why this should be so. God never puts any greater burden upon us than we are able to bear, with the help he is ready to give. Christ stands ever close beside us, willing to carry the heaviest end of every load that is laid upon us.

Men never break down—so long as they keep a happy, joyous heart. It is the sad heart which tires. Whatever our load, we should always keep a songful spirit in our breast. There are two ways of meeting hard experiences. One way is to struggle and resist, refusing to yield. The result is, the wounding of the soul and the intensifying of the hardness. The other way is sweetly to accept the circumstances or the restraints, to make the best of them, and to endure them songfully and cheerfully. Those who live in the first of these ways grow old at mid-life. Those who take the other way of life keep a young, happy heart even to old age.

The true way to live—is to yield to no burden; to carry the heaviest load with courage and gladness; never to let one's eyes be turned downward toward the earth—but to keep them ever lifted up to the hills. Men whose work requires them to stoop all the time—to work in a bent posture—every now and then may be seen straightening themselves up, taking a long, deep breath of air, and looking up toward the skies. Thus their bodies are preserved in health and erectness, in spite of their work. Whatever our toil or burden, we should train ourselves to look often upward, to stand erect, and get a frequent glimpse of the sky of God's love, and a frequent breath of heaven's pure, sweet air. Thus we shall keep our souls erect under the heaviest load of work or care.

The miracle of the straightening of the woman who was bent double, has its gospel of precious hope for any who have failed to learn earlier the lesson of keeping straight. The bowed down may yet be lifted up. The curvature of eighteen years' growth and stiffening was cured in a moment. The woman who for so long had not been able to look up, went away with her eyes upturned to God in praise.

The same miracle Christ is able to work now upon souls that are bent, whether by sin, by sorrow, or by life's load of toil. He can undo sin's terrible work, and restore the divine image to the soul. He can give such comfort to the sad heart—that eyes long downcast shall be lifted up to look upon God's face in loving submission and joy. He can put such songs into the hearts of the weary and overwrought, that the crooked form shall grow straight, and brightness shall come again into the tired face.

Chapter 9. Transfigured Lives.

Every Christian's life should be transfigured. There is a sense in which even a true believer's body becomes transfigured. We have all seen faces that appeared to shine as if there were some hidden light behind them. There are some old people who have learned well, life's lessons of patience, peace, contentment, love, trust, and hope, and whose faces really glow as they near the sunset gates. Sometimes it is a saintly sufferer, who, in long endurance of pain, learns to lie on Christ's bosom in sweet unmurmuring quiet, and whose features take upon themselves increasingly the brightness of holy peace.

But whatever grace may do for the *body*, it always transfigures the *character*. The love of God finds us ruined sinners—and leaves us glorified saints. We are predestinated "to be conformed to the image of his Son." Nor are we to wait for death to transform us; the work should begin at once. We have a responsibility, too, in this work. The sculptor takes the blackened marble block and hews it into a form of beauty. The marble is passive in his hands, and does nothing but submit to be cut and hewn and polished as he will. But we are not insensate marble; we have a part in the fashioning of our lives into spiritual holiness. We will never become like Christ without our own desire and effort.

We ought to know well what our part is, what we have to do with our own sanctification. How, then, may we become transfigured Christians?

There is a transfiguring power in *prayer*. It was as our Lord was praying, that the fashion of his countenance was altered. What is prayer? It is far more than the tame saying over of certain forms of devotion. It is the pouring out of the heart's deepest cravings. It is the highest act of which the soul is capable. When you pray truly, all that is best, noblest, most exalted, purest, heavenliest in you—presses up toward God! Hence earnest prayer always lights up the very face, and lifts up the life into higher, holier mood. We grow toward that which we much desire. Hence prayers for Christ-likeness have a transfiguring effect.

Holy thoughts in the heart have also a transfiguring influence on the life. "As he thinks in his heart—so is he." If we allow jealousies, envies, ugly tempers, pride, and other evil things to stay in our heart—our life will grow into the likeness of these unlovely things. But if we nourish pure, gentle, unselfish, holy thoughts and feelings—our life will become beautiful.

Drummond tells of a young girl whose character ripened into rare loveliness. Her friends watched her growing gentleness and heavenliness with wonder. They could not understand the secret of it. She wore about her neck a little locket within which no one was allowed to look. Once, however, she was very ill, and one of her companions was permitted then to open this sacred ornament, and she saw there the words, "Whom having not seen I love." This was the secret. It was love for the unseen Christ, which transfigured her life. If we think continually of the Christ, meditating upon him, thinking over sweet thoughts of him, and letting his love dwell within us—we shall grow like him.

Communion with Christ transfigures a life. Everyone we meet leaves a touch upon us which becomes part of our character. Our lives are like sheets of paper, and everyone who comes writes a word, or a line, or leaves a little picture painted there. Our intimate companions and friends, who are very close to us, and are much with us, entering into our inner heart-life, make very deep impressions upon us.

If, therefore, we live with Christ, abide in him, the close, continued companionship with him will change us into his likeness. Personal friendship with Christ in this world, is as possible as any merely human friendship. The companionship is spiritual—but it is real. The devout Christian has no other friend who enters so fully into his life as does the Lord Christ Jesus. The effect of this companionship is the transfiguring of the character. It is not without reason that the artists paint the beloved disciple as likest his Lord in features. He knew Jesus more intimately than any of the other disciples, and, in his deeper, closer companionship, was more affected and impressed by the Lord's beauty of holiness.

Again, keeping the eye upon the likeness of Christ, transfigures the life. Gazing by faith upon Christ, the lines of his beauty indeed print themselves on our hearts. This is the meaning of Paul's word: "We all, with unveiled face, beholding as in a mirror the glory of the Lord, are transformed into the same image." The Gospel is the mirror. There we see the image of Christ. If we earnestly, continually, and lovingly behold it, the effect will be the changing of our own lives into the same likeness. The transformation is wrought by the divine Spirit, and our part is only to behold, to continue beholding, the blessed beauty.

There is a touching story of a French sculptor, which illustrates the sacredness with which life's ideal should be cherished and guarded. He was a genius, and was at work on his masterpiece. But he was a poor man, and lived in a small garret, which was studio, workshop, and bedroom to him. He had his statue almost finished, in clay, when one night there came suddenly a great frost over the city. The sculptor lay on his bed, with his statue before him in the center of the fireless room. As the chill air came down upon him, he knew that in the intense cold there was danger that the water in the interstices of the clay would freeze and destroy his precious work. So the old man arose from his bed, and took the clothes that had covered him in his sleep, and reverently wrapped them about his statue to save it, then lay down himself in the cold, uncovered. In the morning, when his friends came in, they found the old sculptor dead; but the image was preserved unharmed.

We each have in our soul, if we are true believers in Christ, a vision of spiritual loveliness into which we are striving to fashion our lives. This vision is our conception of the character of Christ. "That is what I am going to be some day," we say. Far away beyond our present attainment as this vision may shine, yet we are ever striving to reach it. This is the ideal which we carry in our heart amid all our toiling and struggling. This ideal we must keep free from all marring or stain. We must save it though, like the old sculptor, we lose our very life in guarding it. We should be willing to die rather than give it up to be destroyed. We should preserve the image of Christ, bright, radiant, unsoiled, in our soul—until it transforms our dull, sinful, earthly life—into its own transfigured beauty.

No other aim in life is worthy of an immortal being. What debasement, then, to let our lives, with all their glorious possibilities, be dragged down into the dust of shame and dishonor! Rather let us seek continually the glory for which we were made and redeemed. "Beloved, now are we children of God, and it is not yet made manifest what we shall be. We know that, when he shall be manifested, we shall be like him; for we shall see him even as he is. And everyone that has this hope set on him purifies himself, even as he is pure."

A drop of water lay one day in a gutter, soiled, stained, polluted. Looking up into the blue of the sky, it began to wish for purity, to long to be cleansed and made crystalline. Its sigh was heard, and it was quickly lifted up by the sun's gentle fingers—up, out of the foul gutter, into the sweet air, then higher and higher; at length the gentle winds caught it and bore it away, away, and by and by it rested on a distant mountain-top, a flake of pure, white, beautiful snow.

This is a little parable, of what the grace of God does for every sinful life that longs and cries for purity and holiness!

Chapter 10. The Interpretation of Sorrow.

There will always be mysteries in sorrow. Men will always wonder what it means. It is impossible for us, with our earthly limitations, to understand it. Even the strongest Christian faith will have its questions, and many of its questions will have to remain unanswered until the horizon of life is widened, and its dim light becomes full and clear in heaven. Meanwhile, however, some of these questions may be at least partially answered, and grief's poignancy in some slight measure alleviated. And surely no smallest gleam of comfort should be withheld from the world that needs comfort so sorely, and cries out so hungrily for it.

Human hearts are the same everywhere. Sorrow's experiences, while strangely diverse, are yet alike in their general features. Wherever we listen to the suppressed voices of grief, we hear the same questions. What has been answer to one, will therefore be answer to thousands more. Recently, in one day, two letters came to me from sorrowing ones, with questions. Whether any comfort was given in the private answers or not, it may be that the mere stating of the questions, with a few sentences concerning each, may be helpful to others who are carrying like burdens.

One of these letters is from a Christian man whose only son has been led into sinful courses, swiftly descending to the saddest depths. The story is too painful to be repeated in these pages. In his sore distress, the father, a godly man, a man of strong faith and noble wisdom, cries out: "What is the comfort even of Christ and the Bible for me? How can I roll this burden of mine upon God?"

In answer to these questions, it must be remembered that there are some things which even the richest, divinest comfort cannot do. For one thing, it cannot take away the pain of grief or sorrow. Our first thought of comfort usually is that it shall lift off our burden. We soon learn, however, that it is not in this way that comfort ordinarily comes. It does not make the grief any less. It does not make our hearts any less sensitive to anguish. "Consolation implies rather an augmentation of the power of bearing the burden, than a diminution of the burden." In this case, it cannot lift off the loving father's heart the burden of disappointment and anguish which he experiences in seeing his son swept away in the currents of temptation. No possible comfort can do this. The perfect peace in which God promises to keep those whose minds are stayed on him, is not a painless peace in any case of suffering. The crushed father cannot expect a comfort which will make him forget his wandering, sinning child, or which will cause him no longer to feel the poignant anguish which the boy's course causes in his heart. Father-love must be destroyed to make such comforting possible, and that would be a sorer calamity than any sorrow.

The comfort in such a grief, is that which comes through faith in God—even in the sore pain. The child was given to God in his infancy, and was brought up as God's child along his early years. Who will say that he may not yet, in some way, at some time, be brought back to God? The daily burden may then daily be laid in the divine hands. The heart's anguish may express itself not in despairing cries—but in believing prayers, inspired by the promises, and kindled into fervency by blessed hope. Then peace will come, not painless peace—but peace which lies on Christ's bosom in the darkness, and loves and trusts and asks no questions—but waits with all of hope's expectancy.

At the same time we are never to forget, while we trust God for the outcome of our disappointments, that *every sorrow has its mission to our life.* There is something he desires it to work in us. What it may be in any particular instance we cannot tell; nor is it wise for us to ask. The wisest, truest thing we can do, is reverently to open our hearts to the ministry of the sorrow, asking God to do his will in us, not allowing us to hinder the beautiful work he would do, and helping us to rejoice even in the grief. The tears may continue to flow—but then with Mrs. Browning we can sing:

"I praise you while my days go on;
I love you while my days go on;
Through dark and death, through fire and frost,
With emptied arms and treasure lost,
I thank you while my days go on."

The other letter referred to is from another father, over whom wave after wave of sorrow had passed. Within a brief space of time, two children were taken away. The one was a son who had entered his professional career, and had large hope and promise for the future—a young man of rare abilities and many noble qualities. The other was a daughter, who had reached womanhood, and was a happy and beloved wife, surrounded by friends and the refinements of a beautiful home, and all that makes life sweet and desirable. Both of these children God took, one soon after the other. The father, a man of most tender affections, and yet of implicit faith in God, uttered no murmur when called to stand at the graves of his beloved ones; and yet his heart cries out for interpretation.

He writes: "In one of your books I find these words: 'Sometimes our best beloved are taken away from us, and our hearts are left bleeding, as a vine bleeds when a green branch is cut from it . . . Here it is that Christian faith comes in, putting such interpretation and explanation upon the painful things, that we may be ready to accept them with confidence, even with rejoicing . . . A strong, abiding confidence that all the trials, sorrows, and losses of our lives are parts of our Father's husbandry, ought to silence every question, quiet every fear, and give peace and restful assurance to our hearts in all their pain. We cannot know the reason for the painful strokes—but we know that he who holds the pruning-knife is our Father. That ought always to be enough for us to know.'"

Having quoted these words, he continues: "Now I do not question the Father's husbandry. I would also 'silence every question' concerning his wisdom and his love. I would not doubt them for a moment. When I found that my only son, my pride and my staff, must die, I prayed with such strong crying and tears as only they can know who are in like circumstances, yet feeling that I could give back to God what he had lent me without a murmur. By his help, I believe even the slightest murmur has been repressed concerning the painful things, and that in some measure I have been ready to accept them with confidence, even with rejoicing. But my faith has not come in, as you suggest, to put 'such interpretation and explanation' upon them, as perhaps I ought to do. Why has God thus dealt with me? Why was a double stroke necessary? Is his dealing with me purely disciplinary? What are the lessons he would teach me? How am I to test myself as to whether his purpose in afflicting me has been accomplished? Or am I not anxiously to inquire concerning the specific lessons—but rather to let him show in due time what he designed? Such questions multiply without answer."

Has not this writer in his own last suggestion stated what should be done by those who are perplexed with questions as to the interpretation of sorrow? They should not anxiously inquire concerning the specific lessons—but rather let God show in due time what he designed. No doubt every sorrow has a mission. It comes to us, as God's messenger, with a message. If we will welcome it reverently, and be still while it gives its message, no doubt we shall receive some benediction.

Yet we must look at this whole matter carefully and wisely. We are in danger of thinking only of ourselves, and of the effect upon us and our life of the griefs which smite us. We think too often of our bereavements, for example, as if God took away the friend, ending his life, just to chasten or punish us. But we have no right to take so narrow a view of God's design in the removal of loved ones from our side. His purpose concerns *them* as well as *us.* They are called away because their work on earth is done, and higher service in other spheres awaits them. To them death is gain, promotion, translation. The event itself, in its primary significance, is a joyous and blessed one. The sorrow which we experience in their removal, is but incidental. God cannot take them home to glory from our side, without giving us pain. But we must not reverse this order and think that the primary end of the calling away of our beloved ones is to chasten *us*—or to cause *us* to suffer. No doubt there is blessing for us as well as for them in their leaving us, since all things work together for good to those who love God; but we unduly exaggerate our own importance when we think of God as laying a beautiful life low in death merely to teach *us* some lesson, or give to *us* some blessing.

When we look at our bereavements in this light, and think of what death means to our beloved ones who have been taken from us, we find new comfort in the thought of their immortality, their release from suffering and temptation, and their full blessedness with Christ. It is selfish for us to forget this—in the absorption of our own grief. Should we not be willing to endure loss and pain—that those dear to us may receive gain and blessing?

Even in life's relationships on the earth, we are continually taught the same lesson. Parents must give up their children, losing them out of the home nest, that they may go forth into the world to take up life's duties for themselves. Then also the separation is painful—but it is borne in the sweet silence of self-denying love. We give up our friends when they are called from our side to accept other and higher places. Life is full of such separations, and we are taught that it is our duty to think of others, bearing our own loss in patience for their sake. Does not the same law of love "that seeks not its own" apply when our beloved ones are called up higher?

Of lessons to be learned in sorrow, the first always is submission. We are told even of our Lord that he "learned obedience by the things which he suffered." This is life's great, all-inclusive lesson. When we have learned this fully, perfectly, the work of sanctification in us is complete.

Then another lesson in all sorrow comes in the softening and enriching of the life in order to greater personal helpfulness. It is sad for us if for any cause we miss this blessed outcome of grief and pain. Christ suffered in all points that he might be fitted for his work of helping and saving men. God teaches us in our sorrow—what he would have us tell others in their time of trial. Those who suffer patiently and sweetly—go forth with new messages for others, and with new power to comfort.

Beyond these two wide, general lessons of all sorrow, it usually is not wise to press our question, "Why is it?" It is better for us so to relate ourselves to God in every time of trial, that we may not hinder the coming to us of any blessing which he may send—but on the other hand, may receive with quiet, sweet welcome whatever teaching, correction, revealing, purifying, or quickening he would give us. Surely this is far better—than that we should anxiously inquire why God afflicts us, why he sent the sorrow to us, just what he wants it to do for us. We must trust God to work out in us—what he wants the grief to do for us. We need not trouble ourselves to know what he is doing.

Mercifully, our old duties come again after sorrow just as before, and we must take these all up, only putting into them more heart, more reverence toward God, more gentleness and love toward man. As we go on, we shall know what God meant the grief to do for us; or if not in this world, we shall in that home of Light, where all mystery shall be explained, and where we shall see *love's lesson* plain and clear in all life's strange writing. There is no doubt that sorrow always brings us an opportunity for blessing. Then we must remember that in this world alone, can we get the good which can come to us only through pain, for in the life beyond death there is to be no sorrow, no tears. An old Eastern proverb says, "Spread wide your skirts when heaven is raining gold." Heaven is always raining gold when we are sitting under the shadow of the cross. We should diligently improve the opportunity, and learn the lessons he would teach and get the blessings he would give, for the time is short.

Chapter 11. Other People.

There are other people. We are not the only ones. Some of the others live close to us, and some farther away. We stand in certain relations to these other people. They have claims upon us. We owe them duties, services, love. We cannot cut ourselves off from them, from any of them, saying that they are nothing to us. We cannot rid ourselves of obligations to them, and say we owe them nothing. So inexorable is this relation to others, that in all the broad earth there is not an individual who has no right to come to us with his needs, claiming at our hand the ministry of love. The other people are our brothers, and there is not one of them that we have a right to despise, or neglect, or hurt, or thrust away from our door.

We ought to train ourselves to think of the other people. We may not leave them out of any of the plans that we make. We must think of their interests and good, when we are thinking of our own. They have rights as well as ourselves, and we must think of these when asserting our own. No man may set his fence a hair's breadth over the line on his neighbor's ground. No man may gather even a grain of his neighbor's wheat, or a cluster of grapes from his neighbor's vine. No man may enter his neighbor's door unbidden. No man may do anything which will harm his neighbor. Other people have inalienable rights which we may not invade.

We owe other people more than their *rights*; we owe them *love*. To some of them it is not hard to pay this debt. They are lovable and winsome. They are thoroughly respectable. They are congenial spirits, giving us in return quite as much as we can give them. It is natural to love these and be very kindly and gentle to them. But we have no liberty of selection in this broad duty of loving other people. We may not choose whom we shall love—if we claim to be Christians. "Let no debt remain outstanding, except the continuing debt to love one another." Romans 13:8

The Master's teaching is inexorable: "If you love those who love you, what credit is that to you? Even 'sinners' love those who love them. And if you do good to those who are good to you, what credit is that to you? Even 'sinners' do that. And if you lend to those from whom you expect repayment, what credit is that to you? Even 'sinners' lend to 'sinners,' expecting to be repaid in full. But love your enemies, do good to them, and lend to them without expecting to get anything back. Then your reward will be great, and you will be sons of the Most High, because he is kind to the ungrateful and wicked. Be merciful, just as your Father is merciful." Luke 6:32-36

The good Samaritan is our Lord's answer to the question, "Who is my neighbor?" and the good Samaritan's neighbor was a bitter enemy, who, in other circumstances, would have spurned him from his presence. Other people may not be beautiful in their character, nor congenial in their habits, manners, modes of life, or disposition; they may even be unkind to us, unjust, unreasonable, in strict justice altogether undeserving of our favor; yet if we persist in being called Christians ourselves, we owe them the love which thinks no evil, which seeks not its own, which bears all things, endures all things, and never fails.

No doubt it is hard to love the other people who hate us. It is not so hard just to let them alone, to pass them by without harming them, or even to pray for them in a way; but to love them—that is a sore test. Other people, though they be our enemies, are not thus taken out of the circle of those to whom we owe love. Our part is always pictured for us in the example of the good Samaritan.

That is, we owe other people *service*. Service goes with loving. We cannot love truly—and not serve. Love without serving is but an empty sentiment, a poor mockery. God so loved the world that he *gave*. Love always gives. If it will not give it is not love. It is measured always by what it will give. The needs of other people are therefore divine commands to us, which we dare not disregard or disobey. To refuse to bless a brother who stands before us in any kind of need, is as great a sin as to break one of the positive commandments of the Decalogue. Indeed, in a sense, it is the breaking of the whole second table of the commandments—the sense of which is, "You shall love your neighbor as yourself."

We like to think there is no sin in mere *not doing*. But Jesus, in his wonderful picture of the Last Judgment, makes men's condemnation turn on not doing the things they ought to have done. They have simply not fed the hungry, not clothed the naked, not visited the sick, not blessed the prisoner. To make these *sins of neglect* appear still more grievous, our Lord makes a personal matter of each case, puts himself in the place of the sufferer who needs it and is not cared for, and tells us that all neglects to give *needed kindness to any,* are shown to him. This divine word gives a tremendous interest to other people, who are brought providentially into the sphere of our life, so that their wants of whatever kind may make appeal to our sympathy and kindness. To neglect them is to neglect Christ. He sends them to us. They represent him. To turn them away is to turn him away.

This matter of serving has multitudinous forms. Sometimes it is poverty which stands at our gate, and monetary help is needed. A thousand times more frequently, however, it is not money—but something else more precious, that we must give. It may be loving *sympathy*. Sorrow is before us. Another's heart is breaking. Money would be of no use; it would be only bitter mockery to offer it. But we can hold to the neighbor's lips, a cup of the wine of love, filled out of our own heart, which will give new strength to the sufferer.

Or it is the anguish of a life struggle, a human Gethsemane, beside which we are called to watch. We can give no actual aid—the soul must fight its battles alone; but we can be as the angel that ministered in our Lord's Gethsemane, imparting strength, and helping the weary struggler to win the victory.

The world is very full of sorrow and trial, and we cannot live among our fellow-men and be true, without sharing their loads. If we are happy we must hold the lamp of our happiness so that its beams will fall upon the shadowed heart. If we have no burden it is our duty to put our shoulders under the load of others. Selfishness must die—or else our own heart's life must be frozen within us. We soon learn that we cannot live for ourselves and be Christians; that the blessings that are given to us are really for other people, and that we are only God's ministers, to carry them in Christ's name to those for whom they are intended.

We begin to felicitate ourselves upon some special prosperity, and the next moment some human need knocks at our door, and we must share our good things with a suffering brother. We may build up our fine theories of taking care of ourselves, of living for the future, of laying up in the *summer of prosperity*—for the *winter of adversity*, of providing for old age or for our children; but ofttimes all these frugal and economic plans have to yield to the exigencies of human need. The love which seeks not its own, plays havoc with life's hard logic, and with the plans of mere *self-interest*. We cannot say that anything is our own, when our brother is suffering for what we can give.

Not a day passes in the commonest experiences of life, in which other people do not stand before us with their needs, appealing to us for some service which we may render to them. It may be only ordinary courtesy, the gentle kindness of the home circle, the patient treatment of neighbors or customers in business relations, the thoughtful showing of interest to old people or to children. On all sides the lives of others touch ours, and we cannot do just as we please, thinking only of ourselves, and our own comfort and good, unless we choose to be false to all the instincts of humanity, and all the requirements of the law of Christian love. We must think continually of other people.

We may not seek our own pleasure in any way, without asking whether it will harm or mar the comfort of some other one. For example, we must think of other people's convenience, in the exercise of our own liberty and in the indulgence of our own tastes and desires. It may be pleasant for us to lie late in bed in the morning, and we may be inclined to regard the habit as only a little amiable self-indulgence. But there is a more serious side to the practice. It breaks the harmonious flow of the household life. It causes confusion in the family plans for the day. It sorely tries the patience of love.

The other day an important committee of fifteen was kept waiting for ten minutes for one tardy member, whose presence was necessary before anything could be done. At last he came sauntering in without even an apology for having caused fourteen busy men a loss of time that to them was very valuable, besides having put a sore strain on their patience and good nature. *We have no right to forget or disregard the convenience of others.* A conscientious application of the Golden Rule, would cure us of all such carelessness.

These are but illustrations of the way other people impinge upon our life. They are so close to us, that we cannot move without touching them. We cannot *speak*, but that our words affect others. We cannot *act* in the simplest things, without first thinking whether what we are about to do will help or hurt others. We are but one of a great family, and we dare not live for ourselves. We must never forget that there are other people.

Chapter 12. The Blessing of Faithfulness.

"Faithful servant" will be the commendation on the judgment-day of those who have lived well on the earth. Not *great deeds* will be commended—but *faithfulness*. The smallest ministries will rank with the most conspicuous, if they are all that the weak hands could do. Indeed, the widow's *two mites* were more in value—than the rich men's large coins.

Yet faithfulness as a measure of requirement is not something that can be reached without effort. It does not furnish a *pillow for indolence*. It is not a letting down of obligation to a low standard, to make life easy. It is indeed a lofty measurement. "You have been faithful" is the highest possible commendation.

It may not be amiss to look a little at the meaning of the word as a standard of moral requirement. In general, it implies *the doing of all our work as well as we can.* All our work includes, of course, our business, our trade, our household duties, all our daily task-work, as well as our praying, our Bible-reading, and our obeying of the moral law. We must not make the mistake of thinking—that there is no piety in the way we do the common work of our trade or of our household, or our work on the farm, or in the mill or store. The faithfulness Christ requires and commends takes in all these things. Ofttimes, too, it would be easier to be faithful in some *great* trial, requiring sublimity of courage, than in the little unpicturesque duties of an ordinary day. Says Phillips Brooks: "You picture to yourself the beauty of bravery and steadfastness. You let your imagination wander in delight over the memory of martyrs who have died for truth. And then some little, wretched, disagreeable duty comes, which is your martyrdom, the lamp of your oil; and if you will not do it, how your oil is spilt! How flat and thin and unilluminated your sentiment about the martyrs runs out over your self-indulgent life!"

It is true, indeed, that even God cannot do our work without us, without our skill, our faithfulness. If we fail or do our little duty negligently, there will be a blank or a blur—where there ought to have been something beautiful. As another says, "The universe is not quite perfect without my work well done."

One man is a *carpenter*. God has called him to that work. It is his duty to build houses, and to build them well. That is, he is required to be a good carpenter, to do the very best work he can possibly do. If, therefore, he does careless work, imperfect, dishonest, slurred, slighted work, he is robbing God, leaving only bad carpentering where he ought to have left good. For even God himself will not build the carpenter's houses without the carpenter.

Or, here is a *mother* in a home. Her children are about her, with their needs. Her home requires her skill, her taste, her refinement, her toil and care. It is her calling to be a godly mother, and to make a true home for her household. Her duty is to do always her very best to make her home beautiful, bright, happy—a fit place for her children to grow up in. Faithfulness requires that she do always such service as a mother, that Jesus shall say of her home-making, "She has done what she could." To do less than her best is to fail in fidelity. Suppose that her hand should slack, that she should grow negligent, would she not clearly be robbing God? For even God cannot make a beautiful home for her children without her.

So we may apply the principle to all kinds of work. The faithfulness which God requires, must reach to everything we do—to the way the child gets its lessons and recites them, to the way the dressmaker and the tailor sew their seams, to the way the blacksmith welds the iron, and shoes the horse, to the way the plumber puts the pipes into the new building and looks after the drainage, to the way the carpenter does his work on the house, to the way the bridge-builder swings the bridge over the stream, to the way the clerk represents the goods, and measures or weighs them. "Be faithful" is the word which rings from heaven in every ear. "Be faithful" is God's word for the doing of every piece of work that any one does. How soon it would put a stop to all dishonesty, all fraud, all scant work, all false weights and measures, all shams, all neglects or slightings of duty, were this lesson only learned and practiced everywhere!

"It does not matter," people say, "whether I do my little work well or not. Of course I must not steal, nor lie, nor commit forgery. These are moral things. But there is no sin in my sewing up this seam carelessly, or in my using bad mortar in this wall, or in my putting inferior timber in this house, or a piece of flawed iron in this bridge." But we need to learn that the moral law applies everywhere—to carpentry, or blacksmithing, or tailoring. We never can get away from this law.

Besides, it does matter, for our neighbor's sake, as well as for the honor of God's law, how we do our work. The bricklayer does *negligent* work on the walls of the chimney flue he is putting in, and one night, years afterward, a spark creeps through that crevice and reaches a wooden beam which lies there, and soon the house is in flames and perhaps precious lives perish. The bricklayer was unfaithful. The foundryworker, in casting the great iron supports for a bridge, is unwatchful for an instant, and a bubble of air makes a flaw. It is buried away in the heart of the beam and escapes detection. One day, years later, there is a terrible disaster. A great railroad bridge gives way beneath the weight of an express train and hundreds of lives are lost. In the inspection, it is testified that a slight flaw in one beam was the cause of the awful calamity which hurled so many lives into eternity. The foundry workman was unfaithful.

These are but suggestions of the duty and of its importance. No work can be of so little consequence, that it matters not whether it be done faithfully or not. *Unfaithfulness in the smallest things is unfaithfulness,* and God is grieved, and possibly sometime, somewhere, disaster may come as the consequence of the neglect. On the other hand, faithfulness is pleasing to God, though it be only in the sweeping well of a room, or the doing neatly of the smallest things in household care. Then faithfulness is far-reaching in its influence. The universe is not quite complete, without each one's little work well done.

The *self-culture* that there is in the mere habit of *faithfulness* is in itself, a rich reward for all our striving. It is a great thing to train ourselves to do always our *best*—to do as nearly perfect work as possible. Said Michael Angelo: "Nothing makes the soul so pure, so pious, as the endeavor to create something perfect; for God is perfection, and whoever strives for it, strives for something that is Godlike." The habit, unyieldingly persisted in, of doing everything with the most *scrupulous conscientiousness*, builds up in the one who so lives—a noble and beautiful character.

Chapter 13. Without Axe or Hammer.

We read of the temple of Solomon, when it was being built, that it was built of stone made ready in the quarry, so that neither hammer nor axe nor any tool of iron was heard in the house while it went up.

So it is, that the great work of spiritual temple-building goes on continually in this world. We are all really *silent builders*. The kingdom of God comes not with observation. The divine Spirit works in silence, changing men's hearts, transforming lives, comforting sorrow, kindling hope in darkened bosoms, washing scarlet souls white as snow! The preacher may speak with the voice of a Boanerges—but the power which reaches hearts is not the preacher's noise; silently the divine voice whispers in the soul its secret of conviction, or of hope, or of strength. The Lord is not in the *storm*, in the *earthquake*, in the *fire*—but in the sound of gentleness, the Spirit's whisper, which breathes through the soul.

Perhaps the best work any of us do in this world, is that which we do without noise. Words give forth sound—but it is not the sounds which do good, which brighten sad faces as people listen, which change tears to laughter, which stimulate hope, which courage into fainting hearts—it is not the *noise* of our words—but the *thoughts* which the words carry. Words are but the chattering messengers which bear the sealed messages; and it is the messages which help and comfort. We may make noise as we work—but it is not our noise which builds up what we leave in beauty behind us. It is life which builds, and life is silent. The force which works in our homes is a silent force—mother-love, father-love, patience, gentleness, prayer, truth, the influences of divine grace.

It is the same in the building up of personal character in each of us. There may be a great deal of noise all about us—but it is in silence that we grow. From a thousand sources come the little blocks that are laid upon the walls—the lessons we get from others, the influences friends exert upon us, the truths our reading puts into our minds, the impressions life leaves upon us, the inspirations we receive from the divine Spirit—ever the builders are at work on these characters of ours—but they work silently, without noise of hammer or axe.

There is another suggestion. Down in the dark quarries, under the city, the men wrought, cutting, hewing, polishing, the stones. They hung their little lamps on the walls, and with their hammers and chisels they hewed away at the great blocks. Months and years passed; then one day there was a grand dedication, and there in the glorious sunshine all the secret, obscure work of those years was seen in its final beauty, amid the joy of a nation. If the men who had wrought in the quarries were present that day, what a joy it must have been to them to think of their work in preparing the great stones for their place in the magnificent building!

Here is a parable. This world is the quarry. We are toiling away in the darkness. We cannot see what good is ever to come out of our lonely, painful, obscure toil. Yet some day our quarry-work will be manifested in the glory of heaven. We are preparing materials now and here for the temple of the great King, which in heaven is slowly rising through the ages. No noise of hammer or axe is heard in all that wondrous building, because the stones are all shaped and polished and made entirely ready in this world.

We are the stones, and the world is God's quarry. The stones for the temple were cut out of the great rock in the dark underground cavern. They were rough and shapeless. Then they were dressed into form, and this required a great deal of cutting, hammering, and chiseling. Without this stern, sore work on the stones, not one of them could ever have filled a place in the temple. At last when they were ready they were lifted out of the dark quarry and carried up to the mountain-top, where the temple was rising, and were laid in their place.

We are stones in the quarry as yet. When Christ saved us—we were cut from the great mass of rock. But we were yet rough and unshapely; not fit for heaven. Before we can be ready for our place in the heavenly temple—we must be hewn and shaped. The *hammer* must do its work, breaking off the roughnesses.
The *chisel* must be used, carving and polishing our lives into beauty. This work is done in the many processes of life. Every sinful thing, every fault in our character— is a rough place in the stone, which must be chiseled off. All the crooked lines must be straightened. Our lives must be cut and hewn, until they conform to the perfect standard of divine truth.

Quarry-work is not always pleasant. If stones had hearts and sensibilities, they would sometimes cry out in sore pain as they feel the hammer strokes and the deep cutting of the chisel. Yet the workman must not heed their cries and withdraw his hand, else they would at last be thrown aside as worthless blocks, never to be built into the place of honor.

We are not stones; we have hearts and sensibilities, and we do cry out ofttimes as the hammer smites away the roughnesses in our character. But we must yield to the painful work and let it go on, or we shall never have our place as living stones in Christ's beautiful temple. We must not wince under the sorrow and affliction.

There is still another suggestion from this singular temple-building. Every individual life has its quarries, where are shaped the blocks which afterward are built into character, or which take form in acts. *Schools* are the quarries, where, through years of patient study, the materials for life are prepared, the mind is disciplined, habits are formed, knowledge is gained, and power is stored. Later, in active life, the temple rises without noise of hammer or axe. *Homes* are quarries where children are trained, where moral truth is lodged in the heart, where the elements of character are hewn out like fair stones, to appear in the life in after days, when it grows up among men.

Then there are the *thought-quarries,* which are in back of what people *see* in every human life. Men must be silent thinkers before their words or deeds can have either great beauty or power.

Extemporaneousness anywhere, is of small value. Glib, easy talkers, who are always ready to speak on any subject, who require no time for preparation, may go on chattering forever—but their talk is only chatter. The words that are worth hearing come out of thought-quarries where they have been wrought ofttimes in struggle and anguish. So it is of all great thoughts. *Thinkers* brood long in the silence and then come forth and their eloquence sways us. So it is with *art*. We look at a fine picture and our hearts are warmed by its wondrous beauty. But do we know the story of the picture? Years and years of thought and of tireless toil lie in back of its enrapturing beauty. Or here is a *book* which charms you, which thrills and inspires you. Great thoughts lie on its pages. Do you know the book's story? The author lived, struggled, toiled, suffered, wept—that he might write the words which now help you. In back of every good life-thought which blesses men, lies a dark quarry where the thought was born and shaped into the beauty of form which makes it a blessing to the world.

Or here is a noble and beautiful *character*. Goodness appears natural to it. It seems easy for the man to be noble and to do noble things. But again the quarry is in back of the temple. Each one's heart is the quarry out of which comes all that the person builds into his life. "As he thinks in his heart so is he." Everything that appears in our lives—comes out of our hearts. All our *acts* are first *thoughts*. The artist's picture, the poet's poem, the singer's song, the architect's building, are thoughts before they are wrought out into forms of beauty. All dispositions, tempers, feelings, words, and acts—start in the heart. If the workmen had quarried faulty stones in the caverns, the temple would have been spoiled. An evil heart, with stained thoughts, impure imaginings, blurred feelings—can never build up a fair and lovely character.

We need to guard our heart-quarry with all diligence, since out of it are the issues of life. The *thoughts* build the life and make the character! White thoughts rear up a beautiful fabric before God and man. Soiled thoughts pile up a stained life, without beauty or honor. We should look well, therefore, to our heart-quarry, where the work goes on in the darkness without ceasing! If all is right there, we need give little concern to the building of character. Diligent heart-keeping, yields a life unspotted from the world.

A little child had been reading the beatitudes, and was asked which of the qualities named in them she most desired. "I would rather be pure in heart," she said. When asked the reason for her choice, she answered: "If I could but have a pure heart, I would then possess all the other qualities of the beatitudes in the one." The child was right. A pure heart will build a beautiful life—a fit temple for Christ. Thinking over God's holy thoughts after him—will make us like God. Thinking habitually about Christ—Christ's beauty will come into our souls and shine in our faces.

Chapter 14. Doing Things for Christ.

If Christ were here, we say, we would do many things for him. The *women* who love him would gladly minister to him as did the women who followed him from Galilee. The *men* who are his friends would work to help him in any ways he might direct. The *children* who are trying to please him would run errands for him. We all say we would be delighted to serve him—if only he would come again to our world and visit our homes. But we can do things for him just as really as if he were here again in human form!

One way of doing this is by *obeying* him. He is our Lord. Nothing pleases him so well as our obedience. It is told of a great philosopher that a friend called one day to see him, and was entertained by the philosopher's little daughter until her father came in. The friend supposed that the child of so wise a man, would be learning something very deep. So he asked her, "What is your father teaching you?" The little maid looked up into his face with her clear eyes and said, "Obedience!" That is the one great lesson our Lord is teaching us. He wants us to learn obedience. If we obey him always, we shall always be doing things for him.

We do things for Christ, which we do through love to him. Obedience without love, does not please him. But the smallest services we can render, if love inspires them, he accepts. Thus we can make the commonest tasks of our lives holy ministries, as sacred as what the angels do. Christ scorns no work that is done in love to him. Most of us have much drudgery in our lives—but even this we can make glorious, by doing it through love for Christ.

Things we do for others in Christ's name, are done for him. We all remember that wonderful "inasmuch" in the twenty-fifth of Matthew. If we find the sick one, or the poor one, and go and minister, as we may be able, as unto the Lord—the deed is accepted as if done to him in person.

There are fathers and mothers who find it hard to provide for their children. It takes all their time and strength, and sometimes they say, "I cannot do any work for Christ, because it takes every moment to earn bread and clothing for my little ones, and to care for them." But Jesus whispers, "Yes; yet your children are mine, and what you do for them you do for me."

There is in a home an invalid who requires all the time and thought of another member of the household in loving attention. It may be an aged parent—needing the help of a child; it may be a child, crippled, blind, or sick—needing all a parent's care; or it may be a brother broken in health on whom a sister is called to wait continually with patient love. And sometimes those who are required thus to spend their days and nights in ministry for others feel that their lives count for nothing in work for Christ. They hear the appeals for laborers and for service—but cannot respond. Their hands are already filled. Yet Jesus whispers, "These for whom you are toiling, caring, and spending time and strength are mine—and in doing for them, you are doing for me just as acceptable work as are those who are toiling without distraction or hindrance in the great open field."

Sometimes the work we do for Christ with purest love fails, or seems to fail of result. Nothing appears to come of it. There are whole lifetimes of godly people that seem to yield nothing. A word ought to be said about this kind of doing for Christ. We are to set it down as true without exception, that no work wrought in Christ's name and with love for him is ever lost. What we, in our limited, short-sighted vision, planned to do, may not be accomplished—but God's purpose goes on in every consecrated life, in every true deed done. The disciples thought that Mary's costly ointment was wasted. So it seemed; but this world has been a little sweeter ever since the breaking of the vase, which let the perfume escape into its common air. So it is with many things that are done, and many lives that are lived. They seem to fail, and there is nothing on the earth to show where they have been. Yet somehow the stock of human happiness is larger and the world is a little better.

Our work for Christ that fails in what we intended, may yet leave a blessing in some other way. A faithful Bible-class teacher through many months visited a young man, a member of her class, in sickness. She read the Bible to him and sang sweet hymns and prayed by his bedside. He was not a Christian and she hoped that he would be led to Christ. But at length he recovered and went out again, unchanged, or even more indifferent than ever to his spiritual interests. All the faithful teacher's work seemed to have been in vain. Then she learned that a frail, invalid girl, living in an adjoining house, had been brought to Christ through the loving work done for the careless scholar. The songs sung by the sick man's bedside, and which seemed to have left no blessing in his heart, had been heard through the thin wall of the house in the girl's sick-room, and had told her of the love of the Savior.

The records of Christian ministry are full of such good work done unintentionally. Failing to leave a blessing where it was hoped a blessing would be received, it blessed some other life. We may not say that any good work has failed, until we know in the last great harvest all the results of the things we have done and the words we have spoken.

Many people die, and see yet no harvest from their life's sowing. They come to the end of their years, and their hands are empty. But when they enter heaven they will find that they have really been building there all the while, that the things that have seemed to leave no result on the earth, have left glorious results inside the gates of pearl.

Then even if the work we do does not itself leave any record, the doing of it leaves a record—an impression—on our own life. There is a word of Scripture which says, "He who does the will of God abides forever." Doing God's will builds up enduring character in us. Every obedience adds a new touch of beauty to the soul. Every true thing we do in Christ's name, though it leaves no mark anywhere else in God's universe, leaves an imperishable mark on our own life. Every deed of unselfish kindness that we perform with love for Christ in our heart, though it blesses no other soul in all the world, leaves its sure benediction on ourselves.

Thousands of years ago, a leaf fell on the soft clay and seemed to be lost. But last summer a geologist in his ramblings broke off a piece of rock with his hammer, and there lay the image of the leaf, with every line, and every vein, and all the delicate tracery, preserved in the stone through these centuries. So the words we speak, and the things we do for Christ today, may seem to be lost—but in the great final revealing the smallest of them will appear, to the glory of Christ and the reward of the doer.

Chapter 15. Helping and Over-helping.

Even kindness may be overdone. One may be too gentle. Love may hold others back from duty, and thus may wreck destinies. We need to guard against meddling with God's discipline, softening the experience that he means to be hard, sheltering our friend from the wind that he intends to blow chillingly. All summer does not make a good zone to live in; we need autumn and winter to temper the heat, and keep vegetation from luxuriant overgrowth. The best thing we can do for others—is not always to take their load or do their duty for them.

Of course we are to be helpful to others. No aim should be put higher in our life-plans than that of personal helpfulness. The motto of the true Christian cannot be other than that of the Master: "Not to be ministered unto—but to minister." Even in the ambition to gather and retain wealth, the spirit of the desire must be, if we are Christians at all—that thereby we may become more helpful to others; that through, or by means of, our wealth—we may be enabled to do larger and greater good. Whatever gift, power, or possession we have that we do not seek to use in this way—is not yet truly devoted to God. *Fruit* is the test of character, and the purpose of fruit is not to adorn the tree or vine—but to feed hunger. Whatever we are, whatever we have, is fruit, and must be held for the feeding of the hunger of others.

Thus personal helpfulness is the aim of all truly consecrated life. In so far as we are living for ourselves—we are not Christians.

There are many ways of helping others. Some people help us in *material* ways. It is a still higher kind of help which we get from those who minister to our *mental* needs, who write the books which charm, instruct, and assist us. Mind is greater than body. Bread, and clothing, and furniture, and houses—will not satisfy our intellectual cravings. *Good books* bring to us inestimable benefits. They tell us of new worlds, and inspire us to conquer them. They show us lofty and noble ideals, and stimulate us to attain them. They make us larger, better, stronger. The help we get from books is incalculable.

Yet the truest and best help any one can give to others is not in material things—but in ways that make them stronger and better. Money is good—when money is really needed. But in comparison with the divine gifts of hope, friendship, courage, sympathy, and love, it is paltry and poor. *Usually the help people need, is not so much the lightening of their burden, as fresh strength to enable them to bear their burden, and stand up under it.* The best thing we can do for another, someone has said, is not to make some things easy for him—but to make something of him.

It is just here that friendship makes most of its mistakes. It over-helps. It helps by ministering relief, by lifting away loads, by gathering hindrances out of the way, when it would help much more wisely by seeking to impart hope, strength, energy. "Our friends," says Emerson, "are those who make us do what we can." Says another writer: "Our real friend is not the man or woman who smooths over our difficulties, throws a cloak over our failings, stands between us and the penalties which our mistakes have brought upon us—but the man or woman who makes us understand ourselves, and helps us to better things." Love is weak, and too often pampers and flatters. It thinks that loyalty requires it to make life easy as possible for the beloved one.

Too often our friendship is most short-sighted in this regard, and most hurtful to those we fervently desire to aid. We should never indulge or encourage weakness in others, when we can in any way stimulate it into strength. We should never do anything for another—which we can inspire him to do for himself. Much parental affection errs at this point. Life is made too easy for children. They are sheltered—when it were better if they faced the storm. They are saved from toil and exertion—when toil and exertion are God's ordained means of grace for them, of which the parents rob them in their over-tenderness. There are children who are wronged by the cruelty and inhumanity of parents, and whose cries to heaven make the throne of the Eternal rock and sway; but there are children, also, who are wronged of much that is noblest and best in their inheritance by the over-kindness of parents.

In every warm friendship, too, there is strong temptation to make the same mistake. We have to be ever on our guard against over-helping. Our aim should always be to inspire in our friend new energy, to develop in him the noblest strength, to bring out his best manhood. Over-helping defeats these offices of friendship.

There is one particular point at which a special word of caution may well be spoken. We need to guard our sympathies, when we would comfort and help those who are suffering or are in trouble of any kind. It may seem a severe thing to say—but illness is ofttimes made worse by the pity of friends. There is in weak natures a tendency to indulge sickness, to exaggerate its symptoms, to imagine that it is more serious than it really is, and easily to succumb to its influence. You find your friend indisposed, and you are profuse in your expressions of sympathy, encouraging or suggesting fears, urging prompt medical help. You think you have shown kindness—but very likely you have done sore injury. You have left a depressing influence behind you. Your friend is disheartened and alarmed. You have left him weaker, not stronger.

It may seem hard-hearted to appear to be unsympathetic with invalids, and those who are slightly or even seriously sick; not to take interest in their complaints; not to say commiserating things to them; but really it is the part of true friendship to help sick people fight the battle with their ills. We ought, therefore, to guard against speaking any word which will discourage them, increase their fear, exaggerate their thought of their illness, or weaken them in their struggle. On the other hand, we ought to say words which will cheer and strengthen them, and make them braver for the fight. Our duty is to help them to get well.

Perhaps the very medicine they need is a glimpse of cheerful outlook. Sick people ofttimes fall into a mood of disheartenment and self-pity which seriously retards their recovery. To sit down beside them then, and fall into their gloomy spirit, listening sympathetically to their discouraged words, is to do them sore unkindness. The true office of friendship in such cases is to drive away the discouragement, and put hope and courage into the sore heart. We must try to make our sick friend braver to endure his sufferings.

Then, even in the sacredness of sorrow, we should never forget that our mission to others is not merely to *weep* with them—but to *help* them to be victorious, to receive their sorrow as a messenger from God, and to bear themselves as God's children under it. Instead, therefore, of mere emotional condolence with our friends in their times of grief, we should seek to present to them the strong comforts of divine love, and to inspire them to the bearing of their sorrow in faith and hope and joy.

So all personal helpfulness should be wise and thoughtful. It should never tend to pamper weakness, to encourage dependence, to make people timid, to debilitate manliness and womanliness, to make parasites of those who turn to us with their burdens and needs. We must take care that our helping does not dwarf any life which we ought rather to stimulate to noble and beautiful growth. God never makes such mistakes as this. He never fails us in need—but he loves us too well and is too wise to relieve us of weights which we need to make our growth healthful and vigorous. We should learn from God, and should help as he helps, without over-helping.

There are a great many people in this world—hundreds of millions. Yet in a sense each one of us is the only one. Each individual life has relations of its own in which it must stand alone, and into which no other life can come. Companionships may be close, and they may give much comfort and inspiration—but in all the inner meaning of life each individual lives apart and alone. No one can live your life for you. No one but yourself can answer your questions, meet your responsibilities, make your decisions and choices. Your relations with God, no one but yourself can fulfill. No one can believe for you. A thousand friends may encircle you and pray for your soul—but until you lift up your own heart in prayer, no communication is established between you and God. No one can get your sins forgiven but yourself. No one can obey God for you. No other one can do your work for Christ, or render your account at the judgment-seat.

In the realm of experience also, the same is true. Each person suffers alone, as if there were no other being in the universe. Friends may stand by us in our hours of pain or sorrow, and may sympathize with us or administer comfort or alleviation—but they enter not really into the experiences. In these we are alone. No one can meet your temptations for you, or fight your battles, or endure your trials. The tenderest friendship, the holiest love, cannot enter into the solitariness in which each one of us lives apart.

This aloneness of life sometimes becomes very real in consciousness. All great souls experience it as they rise out of and above the common mass of men in their thoughts and hopes and aspirations, as the mountains rise from the level of the valley and little hills. All great leaders of men ofttimes must stand alone, as they move in advance of the ranks of their followers. The battles of truth and of progress have usually been fought by lonely souls. Elijah, for example, in a season of disheartenment and despondency, gave it as part of the exceptional burden of his life, that he was the only one in the field for God. It is so in all great epochs; God calls one man to stand for him.

But the experience is not that only of great souls; there come times in the lives of all who are living faithfully and worthily—when they must stand alone for God, without companionship, perhaps without sympathy or encouragement. Here is a young person, the only one of his family who has confessed Christ. He takes him as his Savior, and then stands up before the world and vows to be his and follow him. He goes back to his home. The members of the home circle are very dear to him; but none of them are Christians, and he must stand alone for Christ among them. Perhaps they oppose him in his discipleship—in varying degrees this ofttimes is the experience. Perhaps they are only indifferent, making no opposition, only quietly watching his life to see if it is consistent. In any case, however, he must stand for Christ alone, without the help that comes from companionship.

Or it may be in the workshop or in the school that the young Christian must stand alone. He returns from the Lord's Table to his week-day duties, full of noble impulses—but finds himself the only Christian in the place where his duty leads him. His companions are ready to sneer, and they point the finger of scorn at him, with irritating epithets. Or they even persecute him in petty ways. They are not Christ's friends, and he, as follower of the Master, finds no sympathy among them in his new life. He must stand alone in his discipleship, conscious all the while, that unfriendly eyes are upon him. Many a Christian finds it very hard to be the only one to stand for Christ in the circle in which his daily work fixes his place.

This aloneness puts upon one a great responsibility. For example, you are the only Christian in your home. You are the only witness Christ has in your house, the only one through whom to reveal his love, his grace, his holiness. You are the only one to represent Christ in your family—to show there the beauty of Christ, the sweetness and gentleness of Christ; to do there the works of Christ, the things he would do if he lived in your home. Perhaps the salvation of all the souls of your family depends upon your being true and faithful in your own place. If you falter in your loyalty, if you fail in your duty—your loved ones may be lost and the blame will be yours; their blood will be upon you.

In like manner, if you are the only Christian in the shop, the store, or the office where you work, a peculiar responsibility rests upon you, a responsibility which no other one shares with you. You are Christ's only witness in your place. If you do not testify there for him, there is no other one who will do it. Miss Havergal tells of her experience in the girls' school at Dusseldorf. She went there soon after she had become a Christian and had confessed Christ. Her heart was very warm with love for her Savior and she was eager to speak for him. To her amazement, however, she soon learned that among the hundred girls in the school, she was the only Christian. Her first thought was one of dismay—she could not confess Christ in that great company of worldly, un-Christian companions. Her gentle, sensitive heart shrank from a duty so hard. Her second thought, however, was that she could not refrain from confessing Christ. She was the only one Christ had there—and she must be faithful. "This was very bracing," she writes. "I felt I must try to walk worthy of my calling for Christ's sake. It brought a new and strong desire to bear witness for my Master. It made me more watchful and earnest than ever before, for I knew that any slip in word or deed would bring discredit on my Master." She realized that she had a mission in that school, that she was Christ's witness there, his only witness, and that she dare not fail.

This same sense of responsibility rests upon every thoughtful Christian who is called to be Christ's only witness in a place—in a home, in a community, in a store, or school, or shop, or social circle. He is Christ's only servant there, and he dare not be unfaithful, else the whole work of Christ in that place may fail. He is the one light set to shine there for his Master, and if his light be hidden, the darkness will be unrelieved. So there is special inspiration in this consciousness of being the only one Christ has in a certain place.

There is a sense in which this is true also of everyone of us all the time. We really are always the only one Christ has at the particular place at which we stand. There may be thousands of other lives about us. We may be only one of a great company, of a large congregation, of a populous community. Yet each one of us has a life that is alone in its responsibility, in its danger, in its mission and duty. There may be a hundred others close beside me—but not one of them can take my place, or do my duty, or fulfill my mission, or bear my responsibility. Though everyone of the other hundred does his work, and does it perfectly, *my* work waits for me, and if I do not do it, it never will be done.

We can understand how that if the great prophet had failed God that day when he was the only one God had to stand for him, the consequences would have been most disastrous; the cause of God would have suffered irreparably. But are we sure that the calamity to Christ's kingdom would be any less if one of us should fail God in our lowly place any common day?

Stories are told of a child finding a little leak in the Holland dike—and stopping it with his hand until help could come, staying there all the night, holding back the floods with his little hand. It was but a tiny, trickling stream that he held back; yet if he had not done it, it would soon have become a torrent, and before morning the sea would have swept over the land, submerging fields, homes, and cities. Between the sea and all this devastation, there was but a boy's hand. Had the child failed, the floods would have rolled in with their remorseless ruin. We understand how important it was that that boy should be faithful to his duty, since he was the only one God had that night to save Holland.

But do you know that your life may be all that stands, between some great flood of moral ruin—and broad, fair fields of beauty? Do you know that your failure in your lowly place and duty may not let in a sea of disaster which shall sweep away human hopes and joys and human souls? The humblest of us dare not fail, for our one life is all God has at the point where we stand.

This truth of personal responsibility, is one of tremendous importance. We do not escape it by being in a crowd, one of a family, one of a community. *No one but ourself can live our life, do our work, meet our obligation, bear our burden!* No one but ourself can stand for us before God to render an account of our deeds. In the deepest, realest sense each one of us lives alone.

There is another phase of this subject, however, which should not be overlooked. While we must stand alone in our place and be faithful to our trust, our responsibility reaches only to our own duty. Others beside us have their part also to do, and the perfection of the whole work, depends upon their faithfulness as well as upon ours. The best any of us can do in this world, is but a fragment. The old prophet thought his work had failed because Baalism was not yet entirely destroyed. Then he was told of three other men, who would come after him—two kings and then another prophet, who each in turn would do his part, when at last the destruction of the great alien idolatry would be complete. Elijah's faithfulness had not failed—but his achievement was only a fragment of the whole work.

This is very suggestive and very comforting. We are not responsible for finishing everything we begin. It may be our part only to begin it; the carrying on and finishing of it may be the work of others whom we do not know, of others perhaps not yet born. We all enter into the work of those who have gone before us, and others who come after us shall in turn enter into our work. Our duty simply is to do well and faithfully our own little part. If we do this we need never fret ourselves about the part we cannot do. That is not our work at all—but belongs to some other worker, waiting now, perchance, in some obscure place, who at the right time will come forward with new heart and skillful hand, anointed by God for his task.

So while we are alone in our responsibility, we need give no thought for anything but our own duty, our own little fragment of the Lord's work. The things we cannot do some other one is waiting and preparing now to do, after the work has passed from our hand. There is comfort in this for any who fail in their efforts, and must leave tasks unfinished which they hoped to complete. The *finishing* is another's mission.

Chapter 17. Swiftness in Duty.

Many good people are very slow. They do their work well enough, perhaps—but so leisurely that they accomplish in their brief time only a fraction of what they might accomplish. They lose, in aimless loitering, whole golden hours which they ought to fill with quick activities. They seem to have no true appreciation of the *value of time*, or of their own accountability for its precious moments. They live conscientiously, it may be—but they have no strong constraining sense of duty impelling them to ever larger and fuller achievement. They have a work to do—but there is no hurry for it; there is plenty of time in which to do it.

It is quite safe to say that the majority of people do not get into their life half the achievement that was possible to them when they began to live, simply because they have never learned to work swiftly, and under pressure of great motives.

There can be no doubt that we are required to make the most possible, of our life. Mr. Longfellow once gave to his pupils, as a motto, this: "Live up to the best that is in you." To do this, we must not only *develop* our talents to the utmost power and capacity of which they are susceptible—but we must also *use* these talents to the accomplishment of the largest and best results they are capable of producing. In order to reach this standard, we must never lose a day, nor even an hour, and we must put into every day and every hour—all that is possible of activity and usefulness.

Dreaming through days and years, however brilliantly one may dream, can never satisfy the demands of the *responsibility* which inheres essentially in every soul that is born into the world. Life means duty, toil, work. There is something divinely allotted to each hour, and the hour one loiters remains forever—an unfilled blank. We can ideally fulfill our mission only by living up always to the best that is in us, and by doing every day the very most that we can do.

We turn over to our Lord for example, since his was the one life in all the ages, which filled out the divine pattern; and wherever we see him, we find him intent on doing the will of his Father, not losing a moment, nor loitering at any task. We see him ever hastening from place to place, from ministry to ministry, from baptism to temptation, from teaching to healing, from miracle-working to solitary prayer. His feet never loitered. He lost no moments; he seems indeed to have crowded the common work of years—into a few short, intense hours. He is painted for us as a man continually under the strongest pressure, with a work to do which he was eager to accomplish in the shortest possible time. He was always calm, never in nervous haste, yet ever quietly moving with resistless energy on his holy errand.

We ought to catch our Master's spirit in this celerity in the Father's business. *Time* is short—and *duty* is large. There is not a moment to lose, if, in our allotted period, we would finish the work that is given us to do. We need to get our Lord's "immediately" into our life, so that we shall hasten from duty to duty, without pause or idle lingering. We need to get into our heart a consciousness of being ever on the Master's errands, that shall be within us a mighty compulsion, driving us always to duty.

Naturally we are indolent, and fond of ease and self indulgence. We need to be carried out of and beyond ourselves. There is no motive strong enough to do this but love to God and to our fellow-men. Supreme love to God makes us desire to do with alacrity, everything he commands. Love to our fellow-men draws us to all service of sympathy and beneficence for them, regardless of cost. Constrained by such motives, we shall never become laggards in duty.

Swiftness or slowness in duty, is very much a matter of habit. As one is trained in early life, one is quite sure to continue in mature years. A loitering child will become a loitering man or woman. The habit grows, as all habits do.

Many people lose in the aggregate whole years of time out of their lives—for lack of *system*. They make no plan for their days. They let duties mingle in inextricable confusion. They are always in feverish haste. They talk continually of being overwhelmed with work, of the great pressure that is upon them, of being driven beyond measure. They always have the air of men who have scarcely time to eat or sleep. And there is nothing feigned in all their intense occupation. They really are hurried men. Yet in the end they accomplish but little in comparison with their great activity, because they work without *order*, and always feverishly and nervously. *Swiftness in accomplishment* is always calm and quiet. It *plans* well, allowing no confusion in tasks. *Hurried haste* is always flurried haste, which does nothing well. "Unhasting yet unresting" is the motto of quick and abundant achievement.

There is another phase of the lesson. Not *swiftness* only—but *patient persistence* through days and years, is the mark of true living. There are many people who can work under pressure for a little time—but who tire of the monotony and slacken in their duty by and by, failing at last because they cannot endure unto the end. There are people who begin many noble things—but soon weary of them and drop them out of their hands. They may pass for brilliant men, men even of genius—but in the end they have for biography only a volume of fragments of chapters, not one of them finished. Such men may attract a great deal of passing attention, while the tireless plodders working beside them receive no praise, no commendation; but in the real records of life, written in abiding lines in God's Book, it is the latter who will shine in the brightest splendor.

So we get our lesson. There is so much to do in our short days—that we dare not lose a moment. Life is so laden with responsibility that to trifle at any point is sin. Even on the seizing of *minutes,* eternal issues may depend. Of course we must take needed rest to keep our lives in condition for duty. But what shall we say of those strong men and women who do almost nothing but rest? What shall we say of those who live only to have amusement, who dance away their nights and then sleep away their days, and thus hurry on toward the judgment-bar, doing nothing for God or for man? Life is duty; every moment of it has its own duty. There is no life so sad and so terrible in its penalties—as that which wastes the golden years in idleness or pleasure, and leaves duty undone.

Shall we not seek to crowd the days with most earnest living? Shall we not learn to redeem the time from indolence, from loitering, from disorderliness, from the waste of precious moments, from self-indulgence, from impatience of persistent toil, from all that lessens achievement? Shall we not learn to work swiftly for our Master?

Chapter 18. The Shadows We Cast.

Everyone of us casts a *shadow.* There hangs about us a strange, indefinable something—which we call *personal influence,* which has its effect on every other life on which it falls. It goes with us wherever we go. It is *not* something we can have when we want to have it, and then lay aside when we will, as we lay aside a garment. It is something that always pours out from our life, like light from a lamp, like heat from flame, like perfume from a flower.

No one can live, and not have influence. Says Burritt: "No human being can come into this world without increasing or diminishing the sum total of human happiness, not only of the present—but of every subsequent age of humanity. No one can detach himself from this connection. There is no sequestered spot in the universe, no dark niche, to which he can retreat from his relations to others, where he can withdraw the influence of his existence upon the moral destiny of the world; everywhere his presence or absence will be felt, everywhere he will have companions who will be better or worse for his influence." These are true words. To be at all—is to have influence, either for good or evil, over other lives.

The ministry of personal influence, is something very wonderful. Without being conscious of it, we are always impressing others by this strange power that goes out from us. Others watch us—and their actions are modified by ours. Many a life has been started on a career of beauty and blessing—by the influence of one noble act. The disciples saw their Master praying, and were so impressed by his earnestness, or by the radiancy they saw on his face, as he communed with his Father, that when he joined them again they asked him to teach them how to pray. Every true soul is impressed continually by the glimpses it has of loveliness, of holiness, or of nobleness in others.

One kind deed, often inspires many kindnesses. Here is a story from a newspaper of the other day, which illustrates this. A little newsboy entered a car on the elevated railway train, and slipping into a cross-seat, was soon asleep. Presently two young ladies came in, and took seats opposite to him. The child's feet were bare, his clothes were ragged, and his face was pinched and drawn, showing marks of hunger and suffering. The young ladies noticed him, and, seeing that his cheek rested against the hard window-sill, one of them arose, and quietly raising his head, slipped her muff under it for a pillow.

The kind act was observed, and now mark its influence. An old gentleman in the next seat, without a word, held out a silver quarter to the young lady, nodding toward the boy. After a moment's hesitation, she took it, and as she did so, another man handed her a dime, a woman across the aisle held out some pennies, and almost before the young woman realized what she was doing, she was taking a collection for the poor boy. Thus from the one little act there had gone out a wave of influence touching the hearts of twenty people, and leading each of them to do something.

Common life is full of just such illustrations of the influence of kindly deeds. Every godly life leaves in the world a twofold ministry, that of the things it does directly to bless others, and that of the silent influence it exerts, through which others are made better, or are inspired to do like godly things.

Influence is something, too, which even death does not end. When earthly life closes, a godly man's active work ceases. He is missed in the places where his familiar presence has brought benedictions. No more are his words heard by those who ofttimes have been cheered or comforted by them. No more do his benefactions find their way to homes of need where so many times they have brought relief. No more does his gentle friendship minister strength and hope and courage, to hearts that have learned to love him. The death of a godly man, in the midst of his usefulness, cuts off a blessed ministry of helpfulness in the circle in which he has dwelt. But his influence continues.

The influence which our dead have over us, is ofttimes very great. We think we have lost them when we see their faces no more, nor hear their voices, nor receive the accustomed kindnesses at their hands. But in many cases there is no doubt that what our loved ones do for us after they are gone, is quite as important as what they could have done for us had they stayed with us. The memory of *beautiful lives* is a benediction, softened and made more rich and impressive by the sorrow which their departure caused. The influence of such sacred memories is in a certain sense—more tender than that of life itself. Death transfigures our loved one, as it were, sweeping away the faults and blemishes of the mortal life, and leaving us an abiding vision, in which all that was beautiful, pure, gentle, and true in him remains to us. We often lose friends in the competitions and strifes of earthly life, whom we would have kept forever had death taken them away in the earlier days when love was strong.

Thus even death does not quench the influence of a godly life. It continues to bless others long after the life has passed from earth.

It must be remembered that not all influence is good. Evil deeds also have influence. Bad men live, too, after they are gone. Cried a dying man whose life had been full of harm to others: "Gather up my influence, and bury it with me in my grave!" But the frantic, remorseful wish was in vain. The man went out of the world—but his bad influence stayed behind him, its poison to work for ages in the lives of others.

We need, therefore, to guard our influence with most conscientious care. It is a crime to fling into the street an infected garment which may carry contagion to men's homes. It is a worse crime to send out a printed page bearing words infected with the virus of moral death. The men who prepare and publish the vile literature which today goes everywhere, polluting and defiling innocent lives, will have a fearful account to render when they stand at God's bar to meet their influence. If we would make our lives worthy of God, and a blessing to the world, we must see to it that nothing we do shall influence others in the slightest degree to evil.

We should keep watch not only over our words and deeds in their *intent* and *purpose*—but also in their *possible influence* over others. There may be liberties which in *us* lead to no danger—but which to *others*, with less stable character and less helpful environment, would be full of peril. It is part of our duty to think of these weaker ones and of the influence of our example upon them. We may not do anything, in our strength and security, which might possibly harm others. We must be willing to sacrifice our liberty, if by its exercise we endanger another's soul. This is the teaching of Paul in the words: "It is better not to eat meat or drink wine or to do anything else that will cause your brother to fall." "Therefore, if what I eat causes my brother to fall into sin, I will never eat meat again, so that I will not cause him to fall."

How can we make sure that our influence shall be only a benediction? There is no way, but by making our life pure and godly. Just in the measure in which we are filled with the Spirit of God and have the love of Christ in us—shall our influence be holy and a blessing to the world.

Chapter 19. The Meaning of Opportunities.

If people's first thoughts were but as good and wise as their after-thoughts, life would be better and more beautiful than it is. We can all see our errors more clearly *after* we have committed them, than we saw them before. We frequently hear people utter the wish that they could go again over a certain period of their life, saying that they would live it differently, that they would not repeat the mistakes or follies, which had so marred and stained the record they had made.

Of course the wish that one might have a second chance with any past period of time, is altogether vain. No doubt there ofttimes is much reason for shame and pain in our retrospects. We live poorly enough at the best, even the saintliest of us, and many of us certainly make sad work of our life. Human life must appear very pathetic, and ofttimes tragic—as the angels look down upon it. There are almost infinitely fewer wrecks on the great sea where the ships go, than on that other sea of which poets write, where lives with their freightage, of immortal hopes and possibilities sail on to their destiny. We talk sometimes with wonder of what the ocean contains, of the treasures which lie buried far down beneath the waves. But who shall tell of the treasures which are hidden in the deeper, darker sea of human life, where they have gone down in the sad hours of defeat and failure?

Glimpses of these lost things—these squandered treasures, these wasted possibilities—these pearls and gems of life that have gone down into the sea of our past—we may have when the reefs are left bare by the refluent tides—but glimpses only can we see. We cannot recover our treasures. The gleams only mock us. The past will not give again its gold and pearls to any frantic appealing of ours.

There is something truly startling in this *irreparableness* of the past, this *irrevocableness* of the losses which we have suffered through our follies or our sins.

In *youth* the hours are full of privileges. They come like angels, holding in their hands rich treasures, sent to us from God, which they offer to us; and if we are laggard or indolent, or if we are too intent on our own little trifles to give welcome to these heavenly messengers with their heavenly gifts, they quickly pass on and are gone. And they never come back again to renew the offer.

On the dial of a clock in the palace of Napoleon at Malmaison, the maker has put, the words, "It does not know how to go backward." It is so of the great clock of Time—it never can be turned backward. The moments come to us but once; whatever we do with them we must do as they pass—for they will never come to us again.

Then *privilege* makes *responsibility*. We shall have to give account to God for all that he sends to us by the mystic hands of the passing hours, and which we refuse or neglect to receive. "They are wasted—and are added to our debt."

The real problem of living, therefore—is how to rightly utilize, what the hours bring. He who does this, will live nobly and faithfully, and will fulfill God's plan for his life. The difference in men is not in the opportunities which come to them—but in their *use* of their opportunities. Many people who fail to make much of their life charge their failure to the lack of opportunities. They look at one who is continually doing good and beautiful things, or great and noble things, and think that he is specially favored, that the chances which come to him for such things are exceptional. Really, however, it is in his capacity for seeing and accepting what the hours bring of duty or privilege, that his success lies. Where other men see nothing, he sees a battle to fight, a duty to perform, a service to render, or an honor to win. Many a man waits long for opportunities, wondering why they never come to him, when really they have been passing by him day after day, unrecognized and unaccepted.

There is a legend of an artist, who long sought for a piece of sandal-wood out of which to carve a Madonna. At last he was about to give up in despair, leaving the vision of his life unrealized, when in a dream he was bidden to shape the figure from a block of oak-wood, which was destined for the fire. Obeying the command, he produced from the log of common firewood, a masterpiece.

In like manner many people wait for great and brilliant opportunities for doing the good things, the beautiful things, of which they dream; while through all the plain, common days—the very opportunities they require for such deeds lie close to them, in the simplest and most familiar passing events, and in the commonest circumstances. They wait to find sandal-wood out of which to carve Madonnas, while far more lovely Madonnas than they dream of, are hidden in the common logs of oak they burn in their open fire-place, or spurn with their feet in the wood-yard.

Opportunities come to all. The days of every life are full of them. But the trouble with too many of us is that we do not make anything out of them while we have them. Then next moment they are gone. One man goes through life sighing for opportunities. If only he had this or that gift, or place, or position—he would do great things, he says; but with his means, his poor chances, his meager privileges, his uncongenial circumstances, his limitations, he can do nothing worthy of himself. Then another man comes up close beside him, with like means, chances, circumstances, privileges, and he achieves noble results, does heroic things, wins for himself honor and renown. The secret is in the *man*—not in his *environment*.

Life is full of illustrations of this. The materials of life which one man has despised and spurned as unworthy of him, as having in them no charmed secret of success, another man is forever picking up out of the dust, and with them achieving noble and brilliant successes. Men, alert and eager, are needed, men with heroic heart and princely hand, to see and use the opportunities that lie everywhere in the most commonplace life.

There is but one thing to do, to get out of life all its possibilities of attainment and achievement; we must train ourselves to take what every moment brings to us of *privilege* and of *duty*. Some people worry themselves over the vague wonder, as to what the divine plan in life is for them. They have a feeling that God had some definite purpose in creating them, and that there is something he wants them to do in this world, and they would like to know how they can learn this divine thought for their life. The answer is really very simple. God is ready to reveal to us, with unerring definiteness, his plan for our life. This revealing he makes as we go on, showing us each moment one little fragment of his purpose. Says Faber: "The surest method of aiming at a knowledge of God's eternal purposes for us, is to be found in the right use of the present moment. Each hour comes with some little fagot of God's will fastened upon its back."

We have nothing to do, therefore, with anything but the privilege and duty of the one hour now passing. This makes the problem of living very simple. We need not look at our life as a whole, nor even carry the burden of a single year; if we but grasp well the meaning of the one little fragment of time immediately present, and do instantly all the duty and take all the privilege that the one hour brings, we shall thus do that which shall best please God and build up our own life into completeness. It ought never to be hard for us to do this.

Living thus we shall make each hour radiant with the radiancy of *duty well done*, and radiant *hours* will make radiant *years*. But the missing of privileges and the neglecting of duties will leave days and years marred and blemished, and make the life at last like a moth-eaten garment. We must catch the sacred meaning of our opportunities if we would live up to our best.

Chapter 20. The Sin of Ingratitude.

A blessing given ought always to have some return. It is better to be a diamond, lighted to shine, than a clod, warmed to be only a dull, dark clod. We all receive numberless favors—but we do not all alike make fitting return.

Krummacher has a pleasant little fable with a suggestion. When Zaccheus was old he still dwelt in Jericho, humble and pious before God and man. Every morning at sunrise he went out into the fields for a walk, and he always came back with a calm and happy mind to begin his day's work. His wife wondered where he went in his walks—but he never spoke to her of the matter. One morning she secretly followed him. He went straight to the tree from which he first saw the Lord. Hiding herself, she watched him to see what he would do. He took a pitcher, and carrying water, he poured it about the tree's roots which were getting dry in the sultry climate. He pulled up some weeds here and there. He passed his hand fondly over the old trunk. Then he looked up at the place among the branches where he had sat that day when he first saw Jesus. After this he turned away, and with a smile of gratitude went back to his home. His wife afterward referred to the matter and asked him why he took such care of the old tree. His quiet answer was, "It was that tree which brought me to him whom my soul loves."

There is no true life without its *sacred memorial* of special blessing or good. There is something that tells of favor, of deliverance, of help, of influence, of teaching, of great kindness. There is some spot, some quiet walk, some room, some book, some face—which always recalls sweet memories. There is something that is precious to us because in some way it marks a holy place in life's journey. Most of us understand that loving interest of Zaccheus in his old tree. In what life is there no place that is always kept green in memory, because there a sweet blessing was received?

Yet there seem to be many who forget their benefits. There is much *ingratitude* in the world. It may not be so universal as some would have us believe. There surely are many who carry in their hearts, undimmed for long years, the memory of benefits and kindnesses received from friends, and who never cease to be grateful and to show their gratitude.

There certainly are unkind hearts—which return coldness for kind deeds. There are children who forget the love and sacrifices of their parents, and repay their countless kindnesses, not with grateful affection, honor, obedience, thoughtfulness, and service—but with disregard, indifference, disobedience, dishonor, sometimes even with shameful neglect and unkindness. There are those who receive help from friends in unnumbered ways, through years, help that brings to them great aid in life—promotion, advancement, improvement in character, widening of privileges and opportunities, tender kindness which warms, blesses, and inspires the heart, and enriches, refines, and ennobles the life—who yet seem never to recognize or appreciate the benefit and the good they receive. They appear to feel no obligation, no thankfulness. They make no return of love for all of love's ministry. They even repay it with complaint, with criticism, with bitterness! We have all known years of continued favors forgotten, and their memory wiped out—by one small failure to grant a new request for help. We have all known malignant hate—to be the return for long periods of lavish kindness.

Ingratitude is robbery! It robs those to whom gratitude is due, for it is the withholding of that which is justly theirs. If you are kind to another, is he not your debtor? If you show another favors, does not he owe you thanks? True, you ask no return, for love does not work for wages. *Only selfishness demands repayment for help given, and is embittered by ingratitude.* The Christlike spirit continues to give and bless, pouring out its love in unstinted measure, though no act or word or look tells of gratitude.

Yet while love does not work for wages, nor demand an equivalent for its services—it is sorely wronged when ungrateful lips are dumb. The quality of ingratitude is not changed because faithful love is not frozen in the heart by its coldness. We owe at least loving remembrance to one who has shown us kindness, though no other return may be possible, or though large return may already have been made. We can never be absolved from the duty of being grateful. "Owe no man anything—but love" is a heavenly word. We always owe love; that is a debt we never can pay off.

Ingratitude is *robbery*. But it is *cruelty* as well as robbery. It always hurts the heart, which must endure it. Few faults or injuries cause more pain and grief in tender spirits, than ingratitude. The pain may be borne in silence. Men do not speak of it to others, still less to those whose neglect or coldness inflicts it; yet It is like thorns in the pillow.

Parents suffer unspeakably when the children for whom they have lived, suffered, and sacrificed, prove ungrateful. The ungrateful child does not know what bitter sorrow he causes the mother who bore him and nursed him, and the father who loves him more than his own life; how their hearts bleed; how they weep in secret over his unkindness. We do not know how we hurt our friends when we treat them ungratefully, forgetting all they have done for us, and repaying their favors with coldness.

There is yet more of this lesson. Gratitude, to fulfill its gentle ministry, must find some fitting expression. It is not enough that it be cherished in the heart. There are many godly people who fail at this point. They are really thankful for the good others do to them. They feel kindly enough in their hearts toward their benefactors. Perhaps they speak to other friends of the kindnesses they have received. They may even put it into their prayers, telling God how they have been helped by his children, and asking him to reward and bless those who have been good to them. But meanwhile they do not in any way express their grateful feelings to the people who have done them the favors, or rendered them the offices of friendship.

How does your friend know that you are grateful—if you do not in some way tell him that you are? Truly here is a sore fault of love, this keeping sealed up in the heart the generous feeling, the tender gratitude, which we ought to speak, and which would give so much comfort if it were spoken in that ear which ought to hear it. No pure, true, loving human heart ever gets beyond being strengthened and warmed to nobler service—by words of honest and sincere appreciation. *Flattery* is contemptible; only vain spirits are elated by it. *Insincerity* is a sickening mockery; the sensitive soul turns away from it in revulsion. But words of true gratitude are always to human hearts—like cups of water to thirsty lips. We need not fear turning people's heads by genuine expressions of thankfulness; on the other hand, nothing inspires such humility, such reverent praise to God, as the knowledge which such gratitude brings—that one has been used of God to help, or bless, or comfort another life.

Silence is said to be golden, and ofttimes, indeed, it is better than speech. "It is a fine thing in friendship," says George MacDonald, "to know when to be silent." There are times when silence is the truest, fittest, divinest, most blessed thing— when words would only mar the hallowed sweetness of love's ministry. But there are times again when silence is disloyalty, cruelty, unkind as winter air to tender plants. Especially is this true of gratitude; to be coldly silent, when the heart is grateful, is a sin against love. When we have a word of thanks in our heart, which we feel we might honestly speak, and which we do not speak, we have sorely wronged our friend.

Especially in homes ought there to be more grateful expression. We wrong *home friends* more than any other friends. Home is where love is truest and tenderest. We need never fear being misunderstood by the loved ones who there cluster about us. Yet too often home is the very place where we are most miserly of grateful and appreciative words. We let gentle spirits starve close beside us—for the words of affectionateness that lie warm in our hearts—yet unspoken, on our tongues. None of us know what joy and strength we could impart to others, if only we would train ourselves to give fitting, delicate, and thoughtful expression to that gratitude which is in our hearts. We would become blessings to all about us, and would receive into our life new gladness.

Nothing is sadder than the sorrow witnessed about many a coffin; the grief of bereavement and loss made bitter by the regret that now the too slow gratitude of the heart, shall never have opportunity to utter itself in the ear which waited so long, hungry, and in vain, for the word that would have given such comfort.

But it is not enough that we be grateful and show our gratitude to the human friends who do us kindnesses. It is to God that we owe all. Every good and perfect gift, no matter how it reaches us, through what messenger, in what form, "comes down from above, from the Father of lights." All the blessings of Providence, all the tender things which come to us through human love and friendship, are God's gifts.

We owe thanks to God, therefore, for all that we receive. When we have shown gratitude to our human benefactors—we still owe our Heavenly Father thanks and gratitude. It is possible, too, for us to be grateful to the friends who help us, and yet be as atheists, never recognizing God, nor giving him any thanks. This is the sorest sin of all. We rob God, and hurt his heart, every time we receive any favor at whatever hand, and fail to speak our praise to him.

Whatever we may say about man's ingratitude to his fellow-men, there is no question about man's lack of gratitude to God. We are continually receiving mercies and favors from him, and yet, are there not days and days with most of us, in which we lift no heart and speak no word in praise? Our prayers are largely requests and supplications for help and favor, with but little adoration and worship. We continue asking and asking, and God continues giving and giving; but how many of us remember always or often—to give thanks for answered prayer?

The angel of *requests*—so the legend runs—goes back from earth heavily laden every time he comes to gather up the prayers of men. But the angel of *thanksgiving*, of *gratitude*, has almost empty hands as he returns from his errands to this world. Yet ought we not to give thanks for all that we receive, and for every answered request? If we were to do this our hearts would always be lifted up toward God in praise.

There is a story of some great conductor of a musical festival suddenly throwing up his baton, and stopping the performance, crying, "Flageolet!" The flageolet was not doing its part and the conductor's trained ear missed its one note in the large orchestra. Does not God miss any voice that is silent in the music of earth that rises up to him? And are there not many voices that are silent, taking no part in the song, giving forth no praise? Shall we not quickly start our heart-song of gratitude, calling upon every power of our being to praise God?

Chapter 21. Some Secrets of Happy Home Life.

Home life ought to be happy. The benediction of Christ on every home to which he is welcomed as an abiding guest is, "Peace be to this house!" While *perfection* of happiness is unattainable in this world, rich, deep, heart-filling happiness certainly may be, and ought to be, attained.

Yet it requires wise building and delicate care to make a *home* truly and sincerely happy. Such a home does not come as a matter of course, by natural growth, wherever a family takes up its abode. Happiness has to be *planned* for, *lived* for, *sacrificed* for, ofttimes *suffered* for. Its price in a home is always the losing of *self*—on the part of those who make up the household. *Home happiness is the incense which rises from the altar of mutual self-sacrifice!*

It may be said, in a word, that **Christ** himself is the one great, blessed, secret of all home happiness; Christ at the marriage altar; Christ when the baby is born; Christ when the baby dies; Christ in the days of plenty; Christ in the pinching times; Christ in all the household life; Christ in the sad hour when farewells must be spoken, when one goes on before and the other stays, bearing the burden of an unshared grief. *Christ is the secret of happy home life!*

But for the sake of simplicity the lesson may be broken up. For one thing, the **husband** has much to do in solving the problem. Does a man think always deeply of the responsibility he assumes when he takes a young wife away from the shelter of mother-love and father-love, the warmest, softest human nest in this world, and leads her into a new home, where his love is to be henceforth her only shelter? No man is fit to be the husband of a true woman, who is not a godly man. He need not be great, nor brilliant, nor rich—but he must be godly, or he is not worthy to take a gentle woman's tender life into his keeping.

Then he must be a man—true, brave, generous, manly. He must be a good provider. He must be a sober man; no man who comes home intoxicated, however rarely, is doing his share in making happiness for his wife and family. He must be a man of pure, blameless life, whose name shall grow to be an honor and a blessing in his household. Husbands have a great deal to do with the matter of happiness at home.

The **wife**, too, has a responsibility. It should be understood at the very beginning, that good housekeeping is one of the first secrets of a happy home. If the man must is a good provider—the woman must be a good home-maker. No woman is ready to marry until she has mastered the fine arts of housekeeping. Home is the wife's kingdom. She holds very largely in her hands, the happiness of the hearts that nestle there. The best husband, the truest, the noblest, the gentlest, the richest-hearted, cannot make his home happy if his wife is not in every sense—a helpmeet. In the last analysis, home happiness does depend on the wife. She is the true home-maker.

Children, too, are great blessings, when God sends them, bringing into the home rich possibilities of happiness. They cost care, and demand toil and sacrifice; ofttimes causing pain and grief: yet the blessing they bring repays a thousand times the care and cost. It is a sacred hour in a home when a baby is born and laid in the arms of a young father and mother. It brings fragments of heaven trailing after it to the home of earth. There are few deeper, purer joys ever experienced in this world—than the joy of true parents at the birth of a child. Much of home's happiness along the years is made by the children. We say we train them—but they train us ofttimes more than we train them. Our lives grow richer, our hearts are opened, our love becomes holier when the children are about us.

Jesus said of little children that those who receive them in his name, receive him. May we not then say that children bring great possibility of blessing and happiness to a home? They come to us as messengers from heaven, bearing messages from God. Yet we may not know their value while we have them. Ofttimes, indeed, it is only the empty crib and the empty arms, which reveal to us the full measure of home happiness that we get from the children. Those to whom God gives children, should receive them with reverence. There are homes where mothers, who once wearied easily of children's noises, sit now with aching hearts, and would give the world to have a baby to nurse, or a frolicking boy to care for. Children are among the secrets of a happy home.

Turning to the life of the household, **affectionateness** is one of the secrets of happiness. There are hundreds of homes in which there is love that would die for its dear ones; and yet hearts are starving there for love's daily bread. There is a tendency in some homes to smother all of love's tenderness, to suppress it, to choke it back. There are homes where the amenities of affection are unknown, and where hearts starve for daily bread. There are husbands and wives between whom love's converse has settled into the baldest conventionalities. There are parents who never kiss their children after they are babies, and who discourage in them as they grow up all longing for caresses. There are homes whose daily life is marred by incessant petty strifes and discourtesies.

These are not exaggerations. Yet there is love in these homes, and all that is needed is that it be set free to perform its sweet ministry. There are cold, cheerless homes which could be warmed into love's richest glow in a little while—if all the hearts of the household were to grow affectionate in expression. Does the busy husband think that his weary wife would not care any longer for the caresses and marks of tenderness with which he used to thrill her? Let him return again for a month to his old-time fondness, and then ask her if these youthful amenities are distasteful to her. Do parents think their grown-up children are too big to be petted, to be kissed at meeting and parting? Let them restore again, for a time, something of the affectionateness of the childhood days, and see if there is not a blessing in it. Many who are longing for richer home happiness, need only to pray for a spring-time of love, with a tenderness that is not afraid of affectionate expression.

We ought not to fear to *speak* our love at home. We should get all the tenderness possible into the daily household life. We should make the morning good-byes, as we part at the breakfast-table, kindly enough for final farewells; for they may be indeed final farewells. Many go out in the morning—who never come home at night; therefore, we should part, even for a few hours, with kindly word, with lingering pressure of the hand, lest we may never look again in each other's eyes. Tenderness in a home is not a childish weakness, is not a thing to be ashamed of; it is one of love's sacred duties. Affectionate expression is one of the secrets of happy home life.

Piety is another of these secrets. It is where the Gospel of Christ is welcomed, that heaven's benediction falls: "Peace be to this house." There may be a certain measure of happiness in a home without Christ—but it lacks something at best, and then when sorrow comes, and the sun of earthly joy is darkened, there are no lamps of heavenly comfort to lighten the darkness. Sad indeed is the Christless home, when a beloved one lies dead within its doors. No words of Christian comfort have any power to console, because there is no faith to receive them. No stars shine through their cypress-trees. But how different it is in the Christian home, in like sorrow! The grief is just as sore—but the truth of immortality sheds holy light on the darkness, and there is a deep joy which transfigures the sorrow.

Then may we not even put **sorrow** down as one of the secrets of happiness in a true Christian home? This may seem at first thought a strange suggestion. But there surely are homes that have passed through experiences of affliction—that have a deeper, richer, fuller joy now, than they had before the grief came. The sorrow sobered their gladness, making it less hilarious—but no less sweet. Bereavement drew all the home hearts closer together. The loss of one from the circle made those that remained, dearer to each other than before. The tears became crystalline lenses, through which faith saw more deeply into heaven. Then in the sorrow Christ came nearer, entering more really into the life of the home. Prayer has meant more since the dark days. There has been a new fragrance of love in the household. There are many homes whose present rich, deep, quiet happiness, sorrow helped to make.

But it is not in sorrow only that piety gives its benediction. It makes all the happiness sweeter to have the assurance of God's love and favor abiding in the household. Burdens are lighter because there is One who shares them all. The morning prayer of the family, when all bow together, makes the whole day fairer; and the evening prayer before sleep, makes all feel safer for the night. Then piety inspires unselfishness, thoughtfulness, the spirit of mutual helpfulness, of burden-bearing, and serving, and thus enriches the home life.

After a while the young folks scatter away, setting up homes of their own. How beautiful it is then to see the old couple, who, thirty or forty years before, stood together at the marriage altar, standing together still, with love as true and pure and tender as ever—waiting to go *home*. By and by the husband goes away and comes back no more, and then the wife is lonesome and longs to go too. A little later and she also is gone, and they are together again on the other side, those dear old lovers, to be parted henceforth nevermore. And that is the blessed end of a happy Christian home.

Chapter 22. God's Winter Plants.

One of the papers tells of a newly discovered flower. It is called the snow-flower. It has been found in the northern part of Siberia. The plant shoots up out of the ice and frozen soil. It has three leaves, each about three inches in diameter. They grow on the side of the stem toward the north. Each of the leaves appears to be covered with little crystals of snow. The flower, when it opens, is star-shaped, its petals being of the same length as the leaves, and about half an inch in width. On the third day the extremities of the anthers show minute glistening specks, like diamonds, which are the seeds of this wonderful flower.

Is not this strange snow-flower, an illustration of many Christian lives? God seems to plant them in the ice and snow; yet they live and grow up out of the wintry cold—into fair and wondrous beauty. We might think that the loveliest lives of earth, are those that are reared amid the gentlest, kindliest influences, under summer skies, in the warm atmosphere of ease and comfort. But the truth is, that the noblest developments of Christian character are grown in the wintry garden of hardship, struggle, and sorrow!

Trial should not, therefore, be regarded with discouragement, as something which will stunt and dwarf the life and mar its beauty. It should be accepted rather, when it comes, as part of God's discipline, through which he would bring out the noblest and best possibilities of our character. Perhaps we would be happier for the time if we had easier, more congenial conditions. Children might be happier without restraint, without family government, without chastening—just left to grow up into all wilfulness and waywardness. But there is something better in life than *present* happiness. Disciplined character in manhood, even though it has been gotten through stern and severe home-training, is better than a childhood and youth of unrestraint, with a worthless manhood as the outcome. A noble life, bearing God's image, even at the price of much pain and self-denial, is better than years of freedom from care and sacrifice with a life unblessed and lost at the end. "To serve God and love him," says one, "is higher and better than happiness, though it be with wounded feet and bleeding hands and heart loaded with sorrow."

It is well that we should understand *how to receive trial* so as to get from its hard experience the good it has for us. For one thing, we should accept it always *reverently*. Resistance forfeits the blessing which can be yielded only to the loving, submissive spirit. Teachableness is the unvarying condition of learning. To rebel against trial is to miss whatever good it may have brought for us. There are some who resent all severity and suffering in their lot as unkindness in God. These grow no better under divine chastening—but instead are hurt by it. When we accept the conditions of our life, however hard, as divinely ordained, and as the very conditions in which, for a time, we will grow the best, we are ready to get from them the blessing and good intended in them for us.

Another important suggestion is that we faint not under trial. There are those who give up and lose all their courage and faith when trouble comes. They cannot endure suffering. Sorrow crushes them. They break down at once under a cross and think they never can go on again. There have been many lives crushed by affliction or adversity, which have not risen again out of the dust. There have been mothers, happy and faithful before, out of whose home one child has been taken, and who have lost all interest in life from that day, letting their home grow dreary and desolate and their other children go uncared for, as they sat with folded hands in the abandonment of their despairing, uncomforted grief. There have been men with bright hopes, who have suffered one defeat or met with one loss, and then have let go in their discouragement and have fallen into the dust of failure, never trying to rise again.

Nothing is sadder in life than such yieldings. They are unworthy of immortal beings. The divine intention in trial never is to crush us—but always to do good to us in some way, to bring out in us new energy of life. Whatever the loss, struggle, or sorrow, we should accept it in love, humility, and faith, take its lessons, and then go on into the life that is before us. When one child is taken out of a home, the mother should, with more reverent heart and more gentle hand, turn the whole energy of her chastened life into love's channels, living more than ever before, for her home and the children that are left to her. The man who has felt the stunning blow of a sudden grief or loss should kiss the hand of God that has smitten—and quickly arise and press onward to the battles and duties before him. We should never accept any defeat as final. Though it be in life's last hours, with only a mere fringe of margin left, and all our past failure and loss, still we should not despair.

There is nowhere any better illustration of the way we should always rise again out of trial, than we have in the life of Paul. From the day of his conversion until the day of his death, trouble followed him. He was misunderstood; he was cast out for Christ's sake; he met persecution in every form; he was shipwrecked; he lay in dungeons; he was deserted by his friends. But he never fainted, never grew discouraged, never spoke one word about giving up. "Cast down—but not destroyed," was the story of his life. He quickly arose out of every trial, every adversity, with a new light in his eye, a new enthusiasm in his heart. He could not be defeated, for he had Christ in him. Shall we not catch Paul's unconquerable spirit, that we may never faint in any trial?

It requires faith to meet trouble and adversity heroically. Undoubtedly, at the time, the blessing is not apparent in the sorrow or the defeat. All seems disastrous and destructive. It is in the future, in the outworking, that the good is to come. It is a matter of faith, not of sight. "All chastening seems for the present to be not joyous—but grievous; yet *afterward* it yields peaceable fruit unto those who have been exercised thereby, even the fruit of righteousness." Oh, the blessing of God's "afterwards"! Jacob one day thought and said that all things were against him—but *afterward* he saw that his great afflictions and losses were wrought in as parts of a beautiful plan of love for him. The disciples thought that the cross was the destruction of all their Messianic hopes; afterward they saw that it was the very fulfillment of these hopes. The *pruning*, which at the time cuts so into the life of the vine, lopping off great, rich branches, afterward is seen to have been the saving and enriching of the whole vine. So we always need faith. We must believe against appearances.

Back and forth the plough was driven. The field was covered with grasses and lovely flowers—but remorselessly through them all the share tore its way, cutting furrow after furrow. It seemed that all the beauty was being hopelessly destroyed. But by and by harvest-time came, and the field waved with golden wheat. That was what the ploughman's faith saw from the beginning.

Sorrow seems to destroy the life of a child of God. Its crude blade ploughs again and again through it, making many a deep furrow, gashing its beauty. But afterward a harvest of blessing and good grows up out of the crushed and broken life. That is what God intends always in trial and sorrow.

Let us have the ploughman's faith, and we shall not faint when the blade is driven through our heart. Then by faith we shall see beyond the pain and trial—the blessing of richer life, of whiter holiness, of larger fruitfulness. And to win that blessing will be worth all the pain and trial.

Chapter 23. Unfinished Life-building.

We are all builders. We may not erect any house or temple on a city street, for human eyes to see—but every one of us builds a fabric which God and angels see. Life is a building. It rises slowly, day by day, through the years. Every new lesson we learn lays a block on the edifice which is rising silently within us. Every experience, every touch of another life on ours, every influence that impresses us, every book we read, every conversation we have, every act of our commonest days—adds something to the invisible building. Sorrow, too, has its place in preparing the stones to lie on the life-wall. All of life furnishes the material.

There are many noble fabrics of character reared in this world. But there are also many who build only low, poor huts, without beauty, which will be swept away in the testing-fires of judgment. There are many, too, whose life-work presents the spectacle of an unfinished building. There was a beautiful plan to begin with, and the work promised well for a little time; but after a while it was abandoned and left standing, with walls half-way up, a useless fragment, open and exposed, an incomplete, inglorious ruin, telling no story of past splendor as do the ruins of some old castle or coliseum—a monument only of folly and failure.

"There is nothing sadder," writes one, "than an incomplete ruin; one that has never been of use; that never was what it was meant to be; about which no pure, holy, lofty associations cling, no thoughts of battles fought and victories won, or of defeats as glorious as victories. God sees them where we do not. The highest tower may be more unfinished than the lowest, to him."

We must not forget the truth of this last sentence. There are lives which to our eyes, seem only to have been begun and then abandoned, which to God's eyes are still rising into more and more graceful beauty. Here is one who began his life-work with all the ardor of youth and all the enthusiasm of a consecrated spirit. For a time his hand never tired, his energy never slackened. Friends expected great things from him. Then his health gave way. The diligent hand lies idle and waiting now. His enthusiasm no more drives him afield. His work lies unfinished.

"What a pity!" men say. But wait! He has not left an unfinished life-work as God sees it. He is resting in submission at the Master's feet and is growing meanwhile as a Christian. The spiritual temple in his soul is rising slowly in the silence. Every day is adding something to the beauty of his character, as he learns the lessons of patience, confidence, peace, joy, love. His building at the last will be more beautiful, than if he had been permitted to toil on through many busy years, carrying out his own plans. He is fulfilling God's purpose for his life.

We must not measure spiritual building by *earthly* standards. Where the heart remains loyal and true to Christ; where the cross of suffering is taken up cheerfully and borne sweetly; where the spirit is obedient though the hands lie folded and the feet must be still—the temple rises continually toward finished beauty.

Or here is one who dies in early youth. There was great promise in the beautiful life. Affection had reared for it a noble fabric of hope. Perhaps the beauty had begun to shine out in the face, and the hands had begun to show their skill. Then death came—and all the fair hopes were folded away. The visions of loveliness and the dreams of noble attainments and achievements, lay like withered flowers upon the grave. An unfinished life! friends cry in their disappointment and sorrow. So it seems, surely, to love's eyes, from the *earth*-side. But it is not so—as *God's* eye looks upon it! There is nothing unfinished, which fulfils the divine plan. God cuts off no young life—until its earthly work is done. Then the soul-building which began here and seemed to be interrupted by death, was only hidden from our eyes by a thin veil, behind which it still goes up with unbroken continuity, rising into fairest beauty in the presence of God.

But there are abandoned life-buildings whose story tells only of shame and failure. Many people begin to follow Christ, and after a little time turn away from their profession, and leave only a pretentious beginning to stand as a ruin to be laughed at by the world, and to dishonor the Master's name.

Sometimes it is *discouragement* which leads men to give up the work to which they have put their hand. Too often noble life-buildings are abandoned in the time of sorrow, and the hands which were quick and skillful before grief came—hang down and do nothing more on the temple-wall. Instead, however, of giving up our work and faltering in our diligence—we should be inspired by sorrow to yet greater earnestness in all duty and greater fidelity in all life. God does not want us to faint under chastening—but to go on with our work, quickened to new earnestness by grief.

Lack of faith is another cause which leads many to abandon their life-temples unfinished. Throngs followed Christ in the earlier days of his ministry when all seemed bright, who, when they saw the shadow of the cross, turned back and walked no more with him. They lost their faith in him. It is startling to read how near even our Lord's apostles came, to leaving their buildings unfinished. Had not their faith come again after their Master arose, they would have left in this world only sad memorials of failure instead of glorious finished temples.

In these very days there are many who, through the losing of their faith, are abandoning their work on the wall of the temple of Christian discipleship, which they have begun to build. Who does not know those who once were earnest and enthusiastic in Christian life, while there was but little opposition—but who fainted and failed when it became hard to confess Christ and walk with him?

Then *sin*, in some form, draws many a builder away from his work, to leave it unfinished. It may be the *world's fascinations*, which draw him from Christ's side. It may be sinful human *companionships*, which lure him from loyal friendship to his Savior. It may be *riches*, which enter his heart and blind his eyes to the attractions of heaven. It may be some secret, debasing *lust*, which gains power over him and paralyzes his spiritual life. Many are there now, amid the world's throngs, who once sat at the Lord's Table and were among God's people. Unfinished buildings their lives are, towers begun with great enthusiasm, and then left to tell their sad story of failure to all who pass by. They began to build—and were not able to finish.

It is sad to think how much of this unfinished work, God's angels see as they look down upon our earth. Think of the *good beginnings* which never come to anything in the end; the excellent resolutions which are never carried out, the noble life-plans entered upon by so many young people with ardent enthusiasm—but soon given up. Think of the beautiful visions and fair hopes which might be made splendid realities—but which fade out, not leaving the record of even one sincere, earnest effort to work them into reality.

In all lines of life, we see these abandoned buildings. The business world is full of them. Men began to build—but in a little time they were gone, leaving their work uncompleted. They set out with gladness—but tired at length of the toil, or grew disheartened at the slow coming of success, and abandoned their ideal when it was perhaps just ready to be realized. Many homes present the spectacle of abandoned dreams of love. For a time the beautiful vision shone in radiance, and two hearts sought to make it come true—but then gave it up in despair.

So life everywhere is full of *beginnings*—never carried out to *completion*. There is not a soul-wreck on the streets, not a prisoner serving out a sentence behind iron bars, not a debased, fallen one anywhere—in whose soul there were not once visions of beauty, bright hopes, holy thoughts and purposes, and high resolves—an ideal of something lovely and noble! But alas! the visions, the hopes, the purposes, the resolves, never grew into more than *beginnings*. God's angels bend down and see a great wilderness of unfinished fabrics, splendid possibilities unfulfilled, noble might-have-beens abandoned, ghastly ruins now, sad memorials only of failure!

The lesson from all this is—that we should finish our work—that we should allow nothing to draw us away from our duty—that we should never weary in following Christ—that we should hold fast the beginning of our confidence, steadfast unto the end. We should not falter under any burden, in the face of any danger, before any demand of cost and sacrifice. No discouragement, no sorrow, no worldly attraction, no hardship, should weaken for one moment our determination to be faithful unto death. No one who has begun to build for Christ, should leave an unfinished, abandoned life-work, to grieve the heart of the Master and to be sneered at as a reproach to the name he bears.

Yet we must remember, lest we be discouraged, that only in a relative, human sense can any life-building be made altogether complete. Our *best* work is *marred* and *imperfect*. It is only when we are in Christ, and are co-workers with him, that anything we do can ever be made perfect and beautiful. But the weakest, and the humblest, who are simply faithful, will stand at last complete in him. Even the merest fragment of life, as it appears in men's eyes, if it is truly in Christ, and filled with his love and with his Spirit—will appear finished, when presented before the divine Presence. To do God's will, whatever that may be, to fill out his plan—is to be complete in Christ, though the stay on earth be but for a day, and though the work done fulfills no great human plan, and leaves no brilliant record among men.

Chapter 24. Iron Shoes for Rough Roads.

The matter of shoes is important. Especially is this true when the roads are rough and hard. We cannot then get along without something strong and comfortable to wear on our feet. One would scarcely expect to find anything in the Bible about such a need as this. Yet it only shows how truly the Bible is fitted to all our actual life to discover in it a promise referring to shoes.

In the blessing of Moses, pronounced before his death upon the several tribes, there was this among other things for Asher: *"Your shoes shall be iron."* A little geographical note will help to make the meaning plain. Part of Asher's allotted portion was hilly and rugged. Common sandals, made of wood or leather, would not endure the wear and tear of the sharp, flinty rocks. There was need, therefore, for some special kind of shoes. Hence the form of the promise: "Your shoes shall be iron."

Bible words, which took the most vivid local coloring from the particular circumstances in which they were originally spoken, are yet as true for us as they were for those to whom they first came. We have only to get disentangled from the local allusions the real *heart* of the meaning of the words, and we have an eternal promise which every child of God may claim.

Turning, then, this ancient promise, into a word for nineteenth-century pilgrims, we get from it some important suggestions. For one thing it tells us that we may have some *rugged pieces of road* before we get to the end of our life-journey. If not, what need would there be for iron shoes? If the way is to be flower-strewn, then velvet slippers would do. No man needs iron-soled shoes for a walk through a soft meadow. The Christian journey is not all easy. Indeed, the Christian life is never easy. No one can live nobly and worthily without struggle, battle, self-denial. One may find *easy* ways—but they are not the *worthiest* ways. They do not lead upward to the noblest things. One reason why many people never grasp the visions of beauty and splendor which shine before them in early years, is because they have not courage for *rough* climbing. We shall need our iron shoes—if we are to make the journey which leads upward to the best possibilities of our life.

But the word is not merely a prophecy of rugged paths; it is also a promise of shoeing for the road, whatever it may be. One who is preparing to climb a mountain, craggy and precipitous, would not put on silk slippers; he would get strong, tough shoes, with heavy nails in the soles. When God sends us on a journey over steep and flinty paths—he will not fail to provide us with suitable shoes.

Asher's portion was not an *accidental* one; it was of God's choosing. Nor is there any accident in the ordering of the *place*, the *conditions*, the *circumstances*, of any child of God's. Our times are in God's hands! No doubt, then, the hardnesses and difficulties of any one's lot—are part of the divine ordering for the best growth of the person's life.

There was a *compensation* in Asher's rough portion. His rugged hills had iron in them. This law of compensation runs through all God's distribution of gifts. In the animal world there is a wonderful harmony, often noted, between the creatures and the circumstances and conditions amid which they are placed. The same law rules in the providence of human life. One man's farm is hilly and hard to till—but deep down beneath its ruggedness, buried away in its rocks, there are rich minerals. One person's lot in life is hard, with peculiar obstacles, difficulties and trials; but hidden in it there are *compensations* of some kind. One young man is reared in affluence and luxury. He never experiences lack or self-denial; he never has to struggle with obstacles or adverse circumstances. Another is reared in poverty and has to toil and suffer privation. The latter seems to have scarcely an equal chance in life. But we all know where the *compensation* lies in this case. It is in such circumstances that grand manhood is grown, while too often the *petted, pampered sons of luxury* come to nothing. In the rugged hills of toil and hardship—life's finest gold is found!

There are few things from which young people of wealthy families suffer more, than from *over-help*. No noble-spirited young man wants life made too easy for him, by the toil of others. What he desires is an opportunity to work for himself. There are some things no other one can give us; we must get them for ourselves. Our *bodies* must grow through our own exertions. Our *minds* must be disciplined through our own study. Our *hearts'* powers must be developed and trained through our own loving and doing.

The best friend we can have, is not the one who digs out the treasure for us—but who teaches and inspires us with our own hands to open the rocks and find the treasures for ourselves. The digging out of the iron—will do us more good than even the iron itself when it is dug out.

Shoes of iron are promised only to those who are to have rugged roads—and not to those whose path lies amid the flowers and soft meadows. There is a comforting suggestion here, for all who find peculiar *hardness* in their life. Peculiar *grace* is pledged to them. God will provide for the ruggedness of their way. They will have a divine blessing which would not be theirs—but for the roughness and ruggedness. The Hebrew parallelism gives the same promise, without figure, in the remaining words of the same verse: "As your days—so shall your strength be." Be sure, if your path is rougher than mine, you will get more divine help than I will. There is a most delicate connection between earth's needs—and heaven's grace. *Days of struggle* get more grace than calm, quiet days. When *night* comes—stars shine out which never would have appeared, had not the sun gone down. *Sorrow* draws *comfort*—which never would have come in joy. For the rough roads—there are iron shoes!

There is yet another suggestion in this ancient promise. The divine blessing for every experience, is folded up in the experience itself, and will not be received in *advance*. The iron shoes would not be given until the rough roads were reached. There was no need for them until then; and besides, the iron to make them was treasured in the rugged hills, and could not be gotten until the hills were reached.

A great many people *worry* about the *future*. They vex themselves by anxious questioning as to how they are going to get through certain anticipated experiences. We had better learn once for all—that there are in the Bible no promises of provision for needs—while the needs are yet future. God does not put strength into our arms today for the battles of tomorrow; but when the conflict is actually upon us—then the strength comes. "As your days—so shall your strength be."

Some people are forever unwisely testing themselves by questions like these: "Could I endure sore bereavement? Have I grace enough to bow in submission to God, if he were to take away my dearest treasure? Or could I meet death without fear?" Such questions are unwise, because there is no promise of grace to meet trial—when there is no trial to be met. There is no assurance of strength to bear great burdens—when there are no great burdens to be borne. Help to endure temptation is not promised—when there are no temptations to be endured. Grace for dying is nowhere promised—while death is yet far off and while one's duty is to live.

There is a story of *shipwreck,* which yields an illustration which comes in just here. Crew and passengers had to leave the broken vessel and take to the life-boats. The sea was rough, and great care in rowing and steering was necessary in order to guard the heavily-laden boats, not from the ordinary waves, which they rode over easily—but from the great cross-seas. Night was approaching, and the hearts of all sank as they asked what they would do in the darkness—when they would no longer be able to see these terrible waves. To their great joy, however, when it grew dark they discovered that they were in phosphorescent waters, and that each dangerous wave rolled up crested with light which made it as clearly visible as if it were mid-day.

So it is that *life's dreaded experiences*, when we meet them, carry in themselves the light which takes away the peril and the terror. The *night of sorrow,* comes with its own lamp of comfort. The *hour of weakness,* brings its own secret of strength. By the brink of the bitter fountain itself, grows the tree whose branch will heal the waters. The *wilderness* with its hunger and no harvest, has daily manna. In dark Gethsemane, where the load is more than mortal heart can bear, an angel appears, ministering strength which gives victory. When we come to the hard, rough, steep path—we find iron for shoes! The iron will be in the very hills, over which we shall have to climb.

So we see that the matter of shoes is very important. We are pilgrims here and we cannot walk barefoot on this world's rugged roads. Are our feet shod for the journey?

"How can I get shoes, and where?" one asks. Do you remember about Christ's feet, that they were pierced with nails? Why was it? That we might have shoes to wear on our feet, and that they might not be cut and torn along the way.

Christ's dear feet were wounded and sore with long journeys over thorns and stones, and were pierced through with cruel nails—that our feet might be shod for earth's rough roads, and might at last enter the gates of heaven, and walk on heaven's gold-paved streets!

Dropping all figure, the whole lesson is that we cannot get along on our life's pilgrimage without Christ; but having Christ we shall be ready for anything which may come to us along the days and years!

Chapter 25. The Shutting of Doors.

The shutting of a door is a little thing—and yet it may have infinite meaning. It may fix a destiny for *weal* or for *woe*. When God shut the door of the ark, the sound of its closing was the knell of exclusion to those who were outside—but it was the token of security to the little company of trusting ones, who were within. When the door was shut behind the bridegroom and his friends who had gone into the festal hall, thus sheltering them from the night's darkness and danger, and shutting them in with joy and gladness—there were those outside to whose hearts the closing of that door issued in their despair and woe. To them it meant hopeless exclusion from all the privileges of those who were within—and exposure to all the sufferings and perils from which those favored ones were protected.

Here we have hints of what may come from the closing of a door. Life is full of illustrations. We are continually coming up to doors which stand open for a little while—and then are shut. An artist has tried to teach this in a picture. *Father Time* is there with inverted hour-glass. A young man is lying at his ease on a luxurious couch, while beside him is a table spread with rich delicacies. Passing by him toward an open door, are certain figures which represent *opportunities*; they come to invite the young man to nobleness, to manliness, to usefulness, to worth. First is a rugged, sun-browned form, carrying a flail. This is *labor*. He invites the youth to toil. He has already passed far by unheeded. Next is a *teacher*, with open book, inviting the young man to thought and study, that he may master the secrets in the mystic volume. But this opportunity, too, is disregarded. The youth has no desire for learning. Close behind the teacher comes a woman with bowed form, carrying a child. Her dress betokens widowhood and poverty. Her hand is stretched out appealingly. She craves *charity*. Looking closely at the picture we see that the young man holds money in his hand. But he is clasping it tightly, and the poor widow's pleading is in vain. Still another figure passes, endeavoring to lure and woo him from his idle ease. It is the form of a beautiful woman, who seeks by love to awaken in him noble purposes, worthy of his powers, and to inspire him for ambitious efforts. One by one these opportunities have passed, with their calls and invitations, only to be unheeded. At last he is arousing to seize them—but it is too late; they are vanishing from sight and the door is closing!

This is a true picture of what is going on all the time in this world. *Opportunities* come to every young person, offering beautiful things, rich blessings, brilliant hopes. Too often, however, these offers and solicitations are rejected—and one by one pass by, to return no more. Door after door is shut, and at last men stand at the end of their days, with beggared lives, having missed all that they might have gotten of enrichment and good, from the passing days.

Take home. A true Christian home, with its love and prayer and all its gentle influences—is almost heaven to a child. The fragrance of the love of Christ fills all the household life. Holiness is in the very atmosphere. The blessings of affection make every day tender with its impressiveness. In all of life, there are no other such opportunities for receiving lovely things into the life, and learning beautiful lessons, as in the days of childhood and youth, which are spent in a home of Christian love. Yet how often are all these influences resisted and rejected. Then by and by the door is shut. The heart that made the home is still in death. The gentle hand that wrought such blessing is cold. Many a man in mid-life would give all he has to creep back for one hour to the old sacred place, to hear again his mother's voice in counsel or in prayer, to feel once more the gentle touch of her hand and to have her sweet comfort. But it is too late. The door is shut.

Take education. Many young people fail to realize what golden opportunities come to them in their school-days. Too often they make little of the privileges they then enjoy. They sometimes waste in idleness the hours they ought to spend in diligent study and helpful reading. They might, if they would, fit themselves for high and honorable places in after years; but they let the days pass with their opportunities. By and by they hear the school door shut. Then, all through their years they move with halting step, with dwarfed life, with powers undeveloped, unable to accept the higher places that might have been theirs if they had been prepared for them, failing often in duties and responsibilities—all because in youth they wasted their school-days and did not seize the opportunities that then came to them for preparation. Napoleon, when visiting his old school, said to the pupils, "Boys, remember that every hour wasted at school means a chance of misfortune in future life." Thousands of failures along the years of manhood and womanhood attest the truth of this monition.

Friendship is another opportunity that offers great blessing. Before every young person stand two kinds of friends, ever reaching out a beckoning hand. The one class whisper of pleasures that lead to sin and debasement. They offer the young man the wine-glass, the gambling-table, the gratification of lust and passion. They offer the young woman flattery, mirthful dress, the dance, pleasures that will tarnish her womanly purity. We all know the end of such friendship.

But there is another class of friends who stand before young people, wooing them to noble things. They may be plain, perhaps homely, almost stern in their earnestness of purpose and in the seriousness with which they talk of life. They call to toil, to diligence, to self-denial, to heroic qualities of character, to purity, to usefulness, to "whatever things are true, whatever things are just, whatever things are honorable, whatever things are lovely." It is impossible to overstate the value of the blessings that true, wise, and worthy friendship offers to the young. It seeks to incite and stimulate them to their best in character and achievement. It would lift them up to lofty attainment, to splendid victoriousness. The young people to whom comes the offer of such friendship are most highly favored.

But how often do we see the blessing rejected for the solicitation of mere idle pleasures which bring no true good, which entangle the life in all manner of complications, which lead into the ways of temptation, and which too often end in disaster and sorrow!

There is a time for the choosing of friends, and when that time is passed and the choice has been made, the door is shut. Then it is too late to go back. There are many people in mid-life, bound now in the chains of evil companionships, who would give all they have for the sweet delights and pure pleasures of friendship which once might have been theirs, which in youth reached out to them in vain, white hands of importunity and blessing. But it is too late; the door is shut.

So it is with the opportunities of **doing good** to others, comforting, helping, cheering, lightening burdens, giving gladness and joy. We stand continually before open doors which we do not enter. Ofttimes we shrink with timid feeling from the sweet ministry, holding back the sympathetic word or restraining ourselves from the doing of the gentle kindness, thinking our offer of love might be unwelcome. Or we do not perceive the opportunity to give a blessing. This is true very often, especially in the closer and more tender intimacies of life. We do not recognize the heart-hunger in our loved ones, and we walk with them day by day, failing to help them in the thousand ways in which we might help them, until they are gone from us and the door is shut. Then all we can do is to bear the *pain of regret*, having only the hope that in some way in the life beyond, we may be able to pay—though so late—love's debt.

These are but illustrations. The same is true in all phases of life. Every day doors are opened for us which we do not enter. For a little time they stand open with bidding and welcome, and then they are closed, to be opened no more forever. To every one of us along our years, there come opportunities, which, if accepted and improved, would fit us for worthy character, and for noble, useful living, and lead us in due time to places of honor and blessing. But how many of us there are who reject these opportunities and lose the good they brought for us from God! Then one by one the doors are shut, cutting off the proffered favors while we go on unblessed.

There is another closing of doors which is even sadder than any of those which have been suggested. There is a shutting of our own heart's door upon God himself. He stands at our gate and knocks and there are many who never open to him at all, and many more who open the door but slightly. The latter, while they may receive blessing, yet miss the fullness of divine revealing which would flood their souls with love; the former miss altogether the sweetest blessings of life.

This sad sound of closing doors, as it falls day after day upon our soul's ears, proclaims to us continually, that something which was ours, which was sent to us from God, and for which we shall have to answer in judgment—is ours no longer, is shut away forever from our grasp. It is a sad picture—the five virgins standing at midnight before a closed door through which they might have entered to great joy and honor—but which to all their wild importunity will open no more. It is sad, yet many of us are likewise standing before closed doors, doors that once stood open to us—but into which we entered not, languidly loitering outside until the sound of the shutting fell upon our ear as the knell of hopeless exclusion: "Too late! Too late! You cannot enter now!"

Of course the past is irreparable and irrevocable, and it may seem idle to vex ourselves in thinking about doors now closed, that no tears, no prayers, no loud knockings, can ever open again. Yes; yet the future remains. The years that are gone we cannot get back again—but new years are yet before us. They too will have their open doors. Shall we not learn wisdom as we look back upon the irrevocable past and make sure that in the future we shall not permit God's doors of opportunity to shut in our faces?

Made in the USA
Las Vegas, NV
05 December 2020